THE LANDSCAPE OF
SCOTLAND

*This book is dedicated with love and thanks to my family.
My parents, Charles and Prim, who have always encouraged my love of
history. Also to Guille, the new generation, in the hope that, whatever he
does, he will carry forward something of a fascination for the world of the past.*

THE LANDSCAPE OF SCOTLAND

A Hidden History

C.R. WICKHAM-JONES

in association with RCAHMS

First published 2001
This edition published 2009

The History Press
The Mill, Brimscombe Port
Stroud, Gloucestershire, GL5 2QG
www.thehistorypress.co.uk

British Library Cataloguing in Publication Data.
A catalogue record for this book is available from the British Library.

ISBN 978 0 7524 1484 3

Typesetting and origination by The History Press
Printed in Great Britain

CONTENTS

LIST OF ILLUSTRATIONS

Text figures

Colour plates

ACKNOWLEDGEMENTS

Many thanks are owed to all of those who have helped to make this book possible. The germ of the book has lain hidden for a long time and several friends have encouraged me not to abandon it. In particular Peter Kemmis Betty of Tempus made it possible for the germ to grow and flower, while Jill Harden provided much advice and encouragement. So too did the staff of the Royal Commission on the Ancient and Historical Monuments of Scotland who took on board my odd idea: Angela Gannon, Strat Halliday, Roger Mercer, Diana Murray, Jack Stevenson, and others, whose encyclopedic knowledge and technical skills aided me in my quest for photographs and encouraged me to stick at it. The staff of the photographic office in RCAHMS must be thanked for the mammoth task of scanning the original photographs onto disc and helping to improve on original clarity. The maps are the work of Kevin H.J. MacLeod and Alan Leith. The text has been read through by Dave Cormie, Jill Harden and Jack Stevenson: their help and encouragement have undoubtedly clarified my ideas and I am very grateful for the time they have spent sorting out my excesses. The responsibility for errors and omissions, of course, rests with the author.

The illustrations are drawn from the collections of the NMRS, and most are copyright of RCAHMS. The following are the non-RCAHMS copyright photographs: Caisteal Gòrach, copyright Dr J. Close-Brooks; Battle Moss, Loch of Yarrows, copyright Roger Mercer; Loch Ard, copyright Stirling Council (thanks to Lorna Main for arranging this); The Cat Stane and Wormy Hillock, Crown Copyright, Historic Scotland (thanks to Dr David Breeze for arranging permission to reproduce these photographs); Bernera Barracks, Churchill Barriers, Den of Boddam, Kinloch, Kilchattan, Orval, copyright the author. I am very grateful to those people who have kindly given permission for me to reproduce their photographs.

NOTE

This book reflects the work of the Royal Commission on the Ancient and Historical Monuments of Scotland as it took place in 2001; although the thrust of their dedication remains unaltered some elements have changed, one of which has been the loss of the name National Monuments Record. Nevertheless, the collections remain an important part of RCAHMS today and are increasingly available through electronic access.

— C.R. Wickham-Jones, 2009

1 INTRODUCTION

I intend this book to provide an introduction to Scottish archaeology through an examination of the monuments that we can find in the countryside. Scotland is well known for its scenery and is well loved by those who care for the land, whether they walk, drive, or dawdle. Today, much of Scotland is considered a wild, 'untamed' land, more or less untouched by her human population. This view is reinforced by the popular use of parts of Scotland to 'get away from it all'. This is not an accurate picture, however. The remoter islands and highlands of Scotland may provide an escape from the pressures of twenty-first-century urbanization, but they have a respectable history of settlement over many millennia, and for those who live in these parts of the country today they provide the basis for the reality of modern life.

Scotland has been inhabited for at least the last 10,000 years, and nowhere has escaped the influence of her past populations. People, over the generations, have left their mark. It is sometimes only a faint trace but it is there, and this book aims to show how that trace may be picked out and understood wherever you are.

Because the book has been put together pictorially, it is not intended to be a comprehensive archaeological textbook. It will not take you in detail through the millennia of Scotland's history from the Mesolithic to the twentieth century. Nor is it intended as a guidebook to the featured sites; those included have been chosen because they are generally representative rather than specifically good to visit. But the book will take you through the main themes of 10,000 years of human activity and it will take you across some of the most beautiful landscapes of Britain. Those who wish to pursue the events of Scottish history in detail can do so in other books (e.g. Armit 1998; Menzies 2001; Mitchison 1982; Ritchie & Ritchie 1992), and a reading list is provided at the end of this volume. Detailed information about individual sites has been kept to a minimum in order to maintain the flow of the text. All of the sites are recorded in the National Monuments Record of Scotland. Information about each site may be freely accessed through CANMORE (Computer Application for National Monuments Record Enquiries; http://www.rcahms.gov.uk), which includes a comprehensive site by site bibliography. CANMORE has formed the basis for most of the site-specific information used in this book.

The illustrations for this book have all come from one source: the National Monuments Record of Scotland (NMRS). Housed in Edinburgh, the NMRS provides a comprehensive library of information on all known Scottish archaeological sites. It does not only contain photos; there are field notes, maps and plans, press cuttings and site reports. It is a veritable treasure house of detail and is open to the public for consultation. Those who are interested in a specific site or area, for example before or after a walk or holiday, can come here to find out more. Abbreviated information is now held on the internet: the NMRS may be consulted over the web (and more information about its work is given in chapter 9). Of course, I have tried to choose the most picturesque photos, but I hope that the following pages will give an idea of the quality of material to be found in the NMRS, as well as of the quality of archaeological remains to be found across Scotland. It was not an easy matter to select pictures for the book from the very many possibles.

In writing this book I have divided up the photographs thematically. The themes are based on a number of basic human needs that have remained constant over the years: for shelter, food, defence and so on. These needs still apply today — our responses to them may be different but they are an important thread by which we are linked with our ancestors. If we explore the past through them it is a useful way to help our understanding of the people who have been here before us. This division is not a simple one, however. Life is complex and therefore archaeology is complex. As we shall see, individual sites do not exist in isolation. People needed somewhere to live as well as somewhere to grow food. Sometimes they needed defence, and they certainly needed a place to bury their dead and venerate their ancestors. There is, of course, considerable overlap between the themes. This is something that is returned to in the conclusions. It requires the skills of many specialists to interpret any one site, and it also demands imagination.

With regard to the individual entries, I have deliberately not chosen glossy, well-preserved sites. These, by and large, are well known, and there are many books that describe them (Breeze 1998; MacSween & Sharp 1989). Many are open to the public, in the care of Historic Scotland. These are well signposted and carefully interpreted for the public. Sites like these, however, comprise only a tiny percentage of our archaeological record. There are many more sites, most of which are less well known to the public in general. I wanted to give the reader an idea of the great archaeological wealth that exists around us, and of the way in which the legacy of the past permeates every nook and cranny that is Scotland today. Many of the sites described here are of great local value, though they may have escaped national notice. This book concentrates on the sort of site that will be encountered on any walk through the countryside, and after reading it I hope that no walk in the country will ever be the same again.

In order to allow readers to follow up individual entries each site name and type is followed by information on the county or island location. There is then a six-figure grid reference which corresponds to the location of the site on an Ordnance Survey (OS) map. The final information corresponds to the number that has been allocated to the site in the archives of the NMRS and in CANMORE. This number also provides information on the OS map sheet on which the site appears. Thus:

Caisteal nan Gillean: Mesolithic shell mound
Oronsay, NR 358 879
NR38NE 8

refers to the site known as Caisteal nan Gillean. It is a Mesolithic shell mound (site type is described and discussed in the caption to each photograph). It is located on Oronsay, and the six figure OS grid reference is NR 358 879. Should you wish to look up further information about the site this could be done through a visit to the NMRS, or on-line through CANMORE. In either case the reference number NR38NE 8 is the one that will lead you to material on that site. The site is recorded in the NMRS on OS map sheet NR38NE.

The sites pictured in this book are mostly in private hands and it is important to remember that this is not a field guide. Some sites have changed dramatically since the photo was taken; a few no longer exist. That does not matter, for the objective of the book is not to lead the reader to any sites in particular, but rather to provide a guide to what certain types of humps and bumps might mean. These sites are not the best of their type, but they are representative. You can come across sites like this anywhere. If you do want to visit any particular site, it is important to get permission from the landowner or tenant, and to remember to respect the Countryside Code. Furthermore, it is important not to damage, or in any way compromise, the well-being of an archaeological site. These sites are the legacy from our past and it is vital that we hand them on to the future. We can learn from them, but not if they have been greatly damaged and disturbed. Many of the sites shown here are protected by law: they are Scheduled Ancient Monuments (Council for Scottish Archaeology, 2001), and it is an offence to damage them in any way. Treasure, by the way, is notably absent from archaeological sites (why else would archaeologists wear torn, faded jumpers and drive around in ancient, muddy, vehicles?). Visible objects, if you should come across them, should be left *in situ* and the local museum or council archaeology service should be notified. Trained archaeologists can learn much from the position of ancient finds in the ground. Archaeologists are trained and equipped to remove pieces from the soil and give them the care and attention that they need. In Scotland, anything old, whatever it be made of — whether metal or stone — is subject to the law of Treasure Trove. This means that finds must be reported to qualified personnel who in turn notify the Treasure Trove Panel, and they decide where it should be housed and whether the finder is due any reward. The interest of any find is greatly enhanced if archaeologists have had the opportunity to investigate the find spot.

For myself, I love learning about the past. It is all around us and I am fascinated by it. I hope, through this book, to inspire a similar love in those who have not had an archaeological education.

Background to Scottish archaeology

This book tries to give an idea of the wide remit that is included within the one heading of archaeology.

Archaeology deals with the physical remains of past human activity. It covers both the ancient past before written records — prehistory — as well as the more recent past which is recorded (albeit patchily) through contemporary writings — history. Archaeological sites may relate to the remote traces of the earliest inhabitants of Scotland, or to recent police boxes and telephone kiosks. We are always adding to the archaeological resource; as the present elements of our culture and activities go out of use so they become a part of archaeology. Our rubbish is tomorrow's archaeological find.

Archaeological remains may be clearly visible, such as a stone circle; they may be scarcely noticeable, such as the low hump of a field bank; or they may be quite invisible on the surface of the ground, such as the buried line of a wall foundation or ditch. Remains include both the traces of settlement and the traces of industry, as well as traces that relate to a host of other activities: for example art, burial, religion, and fortification. Archaeological remains may be well preserved, or almost completely destroyed. Archaeological sites are like icebergs in that what you see above the surface is only ever a small proportion of what survives below ground. For this reason, many archaeological sites are particularly vulnerable to modern development which may easily destroy the vestiges of a site that survived only below the ground.

Furthermore, it is important to remember that archaeological sites can occur underwater, in both freshwater lochs and rivers, as well as in the sea. Our ancestors did not restrict their activities to dry land, nor is the archaeological heritage restricted thus. In certain cases water levels have changed, drowning what were once waterside lands. This applies especially to the traces of some of the earliest settlements in Scotland, 6-8000 years ago. At that time coastal resources were particularly important, so many settlements were sited by the sea. Since then, however, there has been considerable global sea level change, but the picture is not a simple one. Sea level change has created a complex pattern of raised shorelines and drowned features. As sea level is also affected by local tilting of the land this pattern varies around the coast of Scotland. In the Western Isles the western coastlands of 8000 years ago now lie underwater. Around the Firth of Forth the waters once extended inland so that the coast of 6000 years ago now lies well inland.

Through time, the population of Scotland has altered. Invasion and intermarriage have worked to provide an ever-changing population base for our country. At the same time, people's concerns have shifted as technology has developed. The emphasis of settlement has moved to reflect both the shifting needs of the people of Scotland and the changing restrictions and opportunities of a dynamic climate. At the beginning of the third millennium AD we are particularly concerned with climate change, and rightly so, but it is important not to lose perspective. Our early ancestors were also dealing with an unstable climate: they saw considerable sea level change; they endured wetter centuries and dryer centuries; and they had to deal with the outcome of catastrophic events, such as distant volcanic eruptions that cast long shadows of atmospheric dust and lowered temperatures on a global scale. Our ancestors shifted their settlement base accordingly — moving away from the coast, or nearer to it; spreading up hill, and then down again — as conditions changed. The ghostly traces of all this have survived. The landscape is dotted with the abandoned remains of agriculture, religious sites, burials, house remains, roads, and workplaces. These all speak for the people to whom Scotland has been home. I hope this book will help those who are interested to understand a little of what they are saying.

It is clear from this that the landscape of Scotland has undergone considerable change. At any one time in the past it has functioned as a living entity, drawn up by its inhabitants into a suite of categories that have blurred into one another: religious; domestic; industrial; recreational. The predominant elements have shifted with time. These categories are all well known today but their past manifestations do not always appear to be so familiar. It is the task of archaeology to provide some interpretation. As the landscape has changed, however, each new layer has impinged on the previous layers so that only certain monuments have survived — to provide, as it were, port-holes through time through which we can view the different chronological stages in the landscape. When visiting a site we can thus use the particular properties of that site to transport ourselves back in time and get a glimpse of the land as it was. This is a specialized task however — our knowledge is all too incomplete, and it requires specialist help to get the most out of the trip. This book is intended to provide some of that help.

2 SETTLEMENTS IN THE LANDSCAPE

Settlement is a prime human need and people have used elements of the landscape to provide for that need since they first came to Scotland. There are few areas of Scotland that have not once been home to someone. The remote and underpopulated areas of today have abundant evidence of previous communities. From the mobile shelters of the communities who crossed the land at the end of the Ice Age, to the robust architecture of more recent years, a tremendous variety of dwellings have been built here. Most past dwellings have long since disappeared, subject to natural decay, redevelopment, or deliberately targeted destruction. Traces of a cross section survive, however, and these give a good idea of the domestic comforts of previous generations.

A quick scan through the photographs in this chapter will show the very great differences in the scale of things at individual settlement sites. In some cases the slight traces of a group of platforms in the slope of a hill have been interpreted as the location of Bronze Age timber round houses (Normangill Rig). Elsewhere upstanding courses of stone work give a good idea of the nature of a nineteenth-century house (Unish). Some sites such as Caisteal nan Gillean preserve almost intimate detail in the form of domestic rubbish: elements from the diet and jewellery can all be picked out. Other houses have survived with very little waste (Cùl a' Bhaile). Archaeologists work together with many different specialists, like soil scientists and architects, to piece together the surviving evidence.

It is interesting to look at people's choice of land for settlement. Our ancestors had different concerns when they sited their houses. Prior to the great drainage operations of the seventeenth century, lowland settlement had to concentrate on the naturally occurring better drained areas. Many remains of settlements therefore lie on the lower slopes and gravel ridges in positions that can seem strange today. Other factors also influenced the home-builders of the past. Dense vegetation and unstable stony topography affected the choices of the early prehistoric communities, while times of improved climate meant that later settlement could sometimes stretch far up the hillsides (Hill of Alyth and Pitcarmick Loch). It is important to be aware that neither the landscape, nor our use of it, are static.

Even in less densely populated times communities were subject to stress. The early inhabitants of Scotland depended on a thorough knowledge of an area to find food and material resources, and in turn this depended on their ability to travel and navigate. This was not always easy in a landscape with much dense woodland. For this reason early settlement often favours coastlands, major waterways, or obvious routeways. In the Iron Age, a variety of factors including land pressure helped to influence the decision to build some homes out over the lochs: crannogs. The building of a crannog cannot have been easy in comparison with house building on land, but the large numbers of crannog sites (Ardanaiseig), show that it must have been worthwhile.

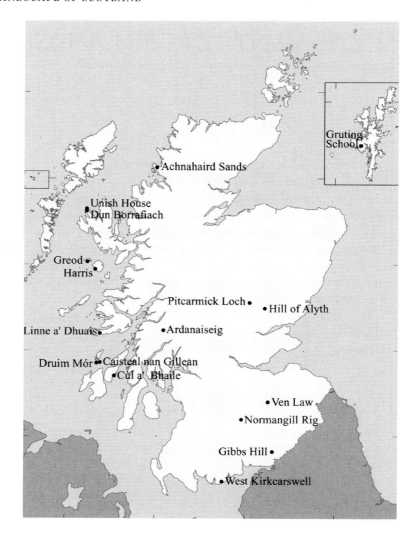

In more recent times the traditionally rural nature of society was undermined by the values of landlords who were driven by outside economics. The clearance of settlement from the Highlands in the late eighteenth and nineteenth centuries is a good example of how the actions of a few could have a major impact on the lives of the majority. As people were moved from their homes so a whole new archaeological chapter was created (Harris on Rum, and Greod on Sanday). At the same time a combination of technological and economic developments meant that people could live together in communities of a size that had never before been imagined. Not only this, there was also a reason for them to do so as they provided the workforce for the industrial revolution. The landscape of Scotland was to become yet more complex with the creation of the first large-scale urban and industrial areas.

Houses are rarely used solely for one purpose. This is as true of the past as it is of today. How many people work from home? Or carry out simple manufacturing tasks such as knitting, sewing and do-it-yourself? For this reason it was sometimes hard to decide where to put a site in this book. The settlement at Achnahaird had strong industrial overtones. Ardanaiseig may well have been defensive in nature (crannogs are also represented in chapter 4 on fortification). Other domestic dwellings with stronger defensive overtones are listed in that chapter only, such as Slack's Tower. It is no easier to compartmentalize life of the past than that of today.

It is also important to remember that Scottish homes today incorporate facilities for many different activities, such as cooking, sleeping and bathing. These have not always been carried out under the same roof. Separate arrangements are found in many different parts of the world today, let alone in the past. It has not been possible to go into great detail on the internal arrangements of each site, but it is important to remember that our ideas of domestic bliss are not necessarily those of others. Mounds of domestic refuse may seem a strange place to live, but for the first inhabitants of Scotland shell mounds such as that at Caisteal nan Gillean made cosy homes. In more recent times the annual division of the community when women and children moved away for several months to the uplands to carry out certain tasks may seem strange (Dun Borrafiach), but we certainly have many habits today that would seem odd to the eyes of the past.

Caisteal nan Gillean: Mesolithic shell mound
Oronsay, NR 358 879
NR38NE 8

The first inhabitants of Scotland arrived just after the end of the last Ice Age, some 10,000 years ago. They were a nomadic Stone Age people who lived by hunting, gathering and fishing. The period is known to archaeologists today as the Mesolithic. People at this time did not build permanent houses or monuments of stone, so Mesolithic remains can be hard to find. Usually only a handful of stone flakes and the scorched remains of a hearth are all that survive of a Mesolithic settlement site as all else has long since been destroyed by Scotland's acid soils. In a few cases, however, remains of domestic rubbish, largely comprising marine shells, have survived. These rubbish sites are known as shell middens. Most shell middens have been preserved in caves and rock shelters but open-air middens have also been found. The tiny island of Oronsay, immediately south of Colonsay in the Inner Hebrides, is well known for a series of five great shell middens which occurs around its coast.

Caisteal nan Gillean is one of the largest of the Oronsay shell middens. All occur as midden mounds — great accumulations of marine shells which have been preserved partly because of the right local conditions and partly because of their very size which has set up micro-environments within them. As a result of their size the middens have long attracted attention: they were noted by Thomas Pennant when he visited Oronsay in 1769. The first recorded investigation of the midden at Caisteal nan Gillean was in 1881 by Symington Grieve and William Galloway. They removed much of the mound and recovered many Mesolithic implements, including stone, bone and antler tools, as well as jewellery made of shell. More recent work has included a project set up by Paul Mellars in the 1970s to investigate both the midden sites and the Mesolithic environment.

Preserved within the midden at Caisteal nan Gillean lie the remains of structures. Patterns of post and stake holes indicate the construction of windbreaks, drying racks, and circular shelters. A midden site is especially valuable for archaeology, however, because of the preservation of organic material. The domestic refuse includes many food remains, and details of the Mesolithic diet can be inferred from the bones and shells. Mammals, fish and birds all formed part of the diet, as did shellfish. Bone tools, as well as the more common stone arrowheads and blades, can provide information on otherwise little-known aspects of Mesolithic life. At Caisteal nan Gillean, for example, there were pieces of antler mattocks and fine bone and antler harpoon heads. Smaller finds include jewellery such as cowrie shell necklaces, and other worked shells such as pecten, which may have served as palettes. Detail of the fauna within the midden gives clues to the Mesolithic landscape and environment, and this can be augmented with fragments of burnt wood and hazelnut shell, as well as pollen grains.

Oronsay today is an open, windswept place. The archaeological research has shown that when it was occupied, around 4000 BC, it would have been quite different. Low thickets of birch and hazel scrub were common, with some oak, as well as willow and alder, growing in damper areas. Sea level was higher by up to 10m and the middens were formed on what was then the shoreline. The investigations show that the marine resources were particularly important to the people who lived there, and so the huge piles of waste developed. As these waste tips grew, so they provided shelter from the on-shore winds. Wind-breaks of skins could be set up on frameworks of stakes and bedded into the mounds for stability, fires were lit, fish were smoked, and a complex sequence of deposition built up. The midden settlements were not occupied permanently: at different times of the year their inhabitants moved elsewhere, but the site marked the location of valuable marine resources and so the people came back, year after year, to leave behind them the mounds that survive today.

Gruting School: Neolithic settlement
Shetland, HU 282 498
HU24NE 9

The remains of four houses dating from the third millennium BC lie on the stony slope by the school at Gruting. House I, in the picture, is the best preserved. Houses II and III have been partially destroyed by the road to the school and by the schoolhouse garage. Today, the remains are well camouflaged on the hillslope, but the stony remains of house I may be seen clearly on the left side of the photograph. The entrance lies on the downhill side, and the house comprised a main chamber, with a smaller chamber to the rear. Only the base of the walls survives, built out of stones and boulders. This would have formed the base for a wall of stone and turf, covered by a low turf roof. There was a hearth inside, and footings from a bench and other internal furnishings were found during excavation in the 1950s. The walls were thick and would have provided considerable insulation against the elements. The main room was some 9m in length, and overall each house would have provided ample living space for a family comprising parents and children, together with some room for grandparents or other relations.

Gruting today appears barren, but 5000 years ago the picture must have been quite different. Scrub woodland would have been relatively common in Shetland, and the remains associated with these houses show that the community were farmers. Small heaps of stones dotted across the hillside around the houses show how the prehistoric farmers

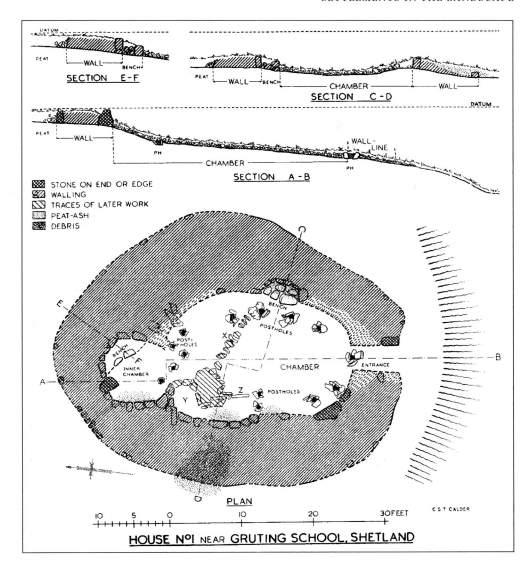

SECTION E-F

SECTION C-D

SECTION A-B

STONE ON END OR EDGE
WALLING
TRACES OF LATER WORK
PEAT-ASH
DEBRIS

PLAN

C S T CALDER

HOUSE Nº1 NEAR GRUTING SCHOOL, SHETLAND

gathered up the boulders from their fields to make tillage easier. The remains of field walls may also be made out, though somewhat obscured by the peat, and there are at least three or four field enclosures. The Neolithic farmers who lived here would not have had an easy life. They tilled their fields using stone ards to tip simple ploughs. They had a few animals — cattle, sheep, and pigs — and they supplemented their harvest with fish and shellfish from the sea. Smoke from the four squat houses would have curled up to the sky, together with the cries of children, noise from the animals, the barking of dogs, and general conversation. Whether it was sowing time or harvest time, the families lived by the rhythm of the seasons. They were not isolated: the community at Gruting must have been frequently in touch with the numerous similar settlements that were scattered across the landscape of Shetland.

Druim Mór: hut-circle
Oronsay, *NR 351 873*
NR38NE 13

The circle in the foreground of the picture marks the site of a hut-circle which marks the spot where a circular house once stood. The remains of the house comprise a stony bank which once formed the base of a wall made of timber or turf, and there would have been a steep conical roof of turf or straw. Hut-circles are commonplace across Scotland, though it often takes a trained eye to spot them. As at Druim Mór the surviving wall footings usually lie hidden below the turf. It is salutary to think that for much of our past round rather than rectangular houses were the norm. Although rectangular structures were certainly known on some Neolithic sites, for some 4000 years, from the Bronze Age onwards, most families preferred round dwellings (3000 BC to AD 1000).

Though they look small on the ground, round houses would have provided ample room for an extended family, and even allowed space for a few animals, such as sheep and cattle, to be brought in for the winter. Excavations at Cùl a' Bhaile on Jura (*NR 549 726, NR57SW 1*) give a good idea of the foundations that lie beneath this type of remains. A broad stone footing was discovered, and inside this a ring of postholes marked out the positions of posts which supported the roof. There was evidence for internal subdivisions and fittings, such as benches and looms. Hut-circles usually had a central hearth, and study has shown that the interior space was often strictly organized and swept clean. There may have been platforms in the roof space to provide additional storage or sleeping areas. Though the popularity of the roundhouse spans several periods, from the Bronze Age through the Iron Age, the way of life of their inhabitants changed little over time. Everyday artefacts were largely made of wood, horn and bone, all of which have long since been dissolved away by Scotland's acid soils. Coarse earthenware pottery was sometimes supplemented by finer wares depending on the wealth and connections of the family. Metal goods were rare, often limited to a single knife. In later periods foreign goods might occasionally appear in areas where contact with outside traders or troops took place.

Hut-circles occur both singly and in groups, sometimes very large groups. They are often surrounded by the remains of the fields and enclosures that made up the farmlands of their inhabitants. At Cùl a' Bhaile the hut-circle lay alone inside an enclosure, and the excavations revealed that the ground where it had been built had previously been ploughed. At Druim Mór the circle also stood alone, just to the north-east of a well-preserved field system comprising several field banks and some 50 clearance cairns, where generations of farmers have piled stones during cultivation. For much of Scotland's past, life for most people has revolved around agriculture.

See **colour plate 1**

Hill of Alyth: ring-ditch house
Perthshire, NO 224 501
NO25SE 29

Ring-ditch houses are a particular type of hut-circle that did not involve a stone footing. The traces of the round house, at Hill of Alyth, stand out clearly as a shallow circular depression with a central platform in the rough pasture at the margins of today's cultivated land. It is one of a pair of ring-ditch houses and seven hut-circles, all set on a terrace on the west flank of the Hill of Alyth. It is impossible to say whether all were inhabited at the same time. A cluster of clearance cairns marks the cultivated fields that went with this small settlement, and there is also a ruinous burial cairn. This settlement is typical of many that dot the hills of Perthshire; in late prehistory, as today, it was a fertile place and apparently well populated.

It is hard to reconstruct the house that stood here from the field evidence alone, so archaeologists use information that they have derived from excavations elsewhere. Like the hut-circle, the ring-ditch marks the spot where a circular house once stood, and both belong to similar periods. The difference in the remains relates to different building traditions. The remains at Hill of Alyth contain no evidence of stone, so it is likely that the house walls were of timber or turf, or a combination of the two. Turf would make a useful insulating material against the Perthshire wind, but other materials such as daub, sheep's wool and vegetation were also sometimes used. Around the outside of the walls a groove built up, or was deliberately dug, to take the run-off from the roof, and lead it away. In this way the interior could be kept dry even in the wettest season.

Inside, the ring-ditch house would be very similar to a hut-circle. It provided snug accommodation for a family, often with some space set aside for animals. There would be an internal hearth and probably some internal wooden partitions, as well as fixed furnishings such as beds and looms. A steep thatch would lead to a smoke hole and this would be the only way in which light entered the dwelling. The interior of prehistoric round houses would seem very dark and gloomy to our eyes, which are accustomed to modern lighting; however, reconstructions, at museums such as Archaeolink, near Aberdeen, have shown that one can quickly get accustomed to working in reduced lighting. It is likely that part of the roof space was floored in with a timber floor supported on the main internal posts to provide additional space.

Ring-ditch houses are typical of many of the traces of the past. There is little sign on the ground surface of the human activity that once took place here. That anything has survived at all of past structures such as these seems amazing given the fragility of the remains and the considerable periods of time that have elapsed since they were in use.

See **colour plate 2**

Normangill Rig: unenclosed platform settlement
Lanarkshire, NS 963 217
NS92SE 25

The picture shows a fairly typical Borders scene of rough pasture and a plantation. Three thousand years ago, however, the landscape here was very different. The photograph is taken from within a small settlement of Bronze Age houses of which all that can be made out today are the scooped, flattened platforms on which they sat.

The Bronze Age farmers of the Borders made use of the higher hillslopes for their settlements and agricultural land. The lower lands had not yet been drained so that many valley bottoms were boggy and harder to clear and farm. At the same time, there was pressure on the available lower land due to an increase in population. The climate at the start of the Bronze Age was slightly better than today making it possible for the farmers to work the higher lands. Only towards the end of the Bronze Age did the climate deteriorate, making life more difficult for the hill farmers. Many settlements such as Normangill Rig were abandoned at this time.

The settlement at Normangill Rig comprised a group of round houses built of wood and turf, with steep conical roofs. The slope of the land meant that the community had to level out individual platforms for each house and it is these platforms that mark the settlement site today. In the photograph a clear platform may be seen up against the

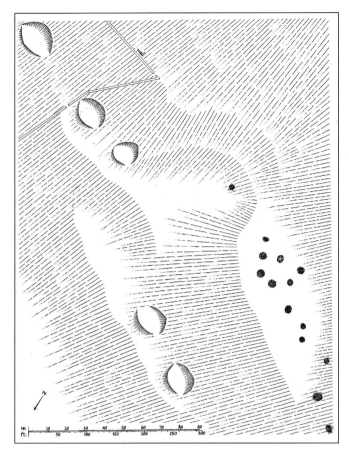

plantation wall and another, less well defined, lies in the right foreground. The village was strung out along the hillside at a height of about 280m OD. At least 22 house platforms have been recorded here, of which the plan shows the middle portion. We cannot be sure that all of these houses were occupied at the same time; change and movement are still a feature of any village today, but we can be sure that a dynamic farming community of several households made its home here.

As the plan shows, the inhabitants of Normangill Rig left other traces besides their houses. Just above the house platforms there is a group of at least 14 clearance cairns where field stones have been piled to ease cultivation. To the north-west of the settlement site the low ring mound of an enclosed cremation cemetery has been recorded on the slopes of Fall Hill, and to the east lies a denuded round burial cairn. From the remains on the ground it is not possible to be certain whether the Bronze Age farmers from Normangill Rig buried their dead in either of these monuments, but they are so close that some association seems likely. Similarly, the flanks of Normangill Rig, above the Midlock Burn, have other evidence for Bronze Age settlement. Two other unenclosed platform settlements from this time have been recorded here. Individual settlements do not exist in isolation and it is part of the archaeologist's job to look at the general world within which our ancestors lived. At Normangill Rig the remains show how the settlement in the picture was only part of the wider Bronze Age world.

Normangill Rig is typical of the fragile archaeological sites that date from the Bronze Age. Though there is little to see, intensive agriculture in more recent times has tended to avoid the higher slopes so that the Bronze Age settlement remains in these locations have been preserved. The picture clearly demonstrates, however, how vulnerable these sites are. Little survives where the trees have been planted and their roots will have done immeasurable damage to the remains preserved below the ground.

Gibbs Hill: Palisaded Settlement
Dumfries and Galloway, NY308 841
NY38SW 13

See **colour plate 3**

The archaeologists in the picture are surveying the settlement on the summit of Gibbs Hill in order to make a detailed plan of the site. The archaeological remains here comprise the traces of a sequence of settlement that dates from the late prehistoric period. In the picture the narrow slots of the palisades that were built to enclose and defend the settlement show up clearly.

The remains on Gibbs Hill consist of a complex series of grooves from the digging of palisade trenches, together with the traces of internal round houses. The sequence of settlement is difficult to work out but it seems that the earliest settlement on the hill took place about 3000 years ago and comprised the construction of an unenclosed homestead consisting of at least two timber round houses. Subsequently, a single timber palisade was erected to enclose an area on the top of the hill. This was remodelled at least once before being elaborated into a double palisaded enclosure. At some time a new, double palisade was built to enclose the settlement, and, in the final phase, a single palisade was used once again. Interestingly, the area enclosed within the palisades got slightly smaller with each rebuilding. Traces of a single entrance to each phase of palisade show clearly on the ground.

The traces of several timber round houses have been recorded within the palisaded area, but it is difficult to work out how many houses were in use at any one time and which houses relate to which phase of the palisades. It would seem that the settlement probably only ever consisted of three or four houses, so the community here was not large. It is typical of the small agricultural communities that existed in later prehistory. The traces of the fields that they cultivated have been recorded to the south-west of the settlement where long parallel lines of ridges, or rigs, mark out the plough furrows. The palisade would have served as much to contain stock and keep out marauding wild animals as to provide a barrier against human enemies, though this was a time of increased neighbourly conflict and it was undoubtedly important to show others that you were quite capable of defending your home and your family.

West Kirkcarswell: homestead
Kirkudbrightshire, NX749 494
NX74NW 5

As might be expected, the fertile lowlands of Scotland have a complex settlement history. Generations of farmers have inadvertently worked to blur, or even obliterate, the signs left by previous occupants, and this has been compounded by the introduction of recent intensive methods of agriculture. Nevertheless, some sites do survive to give us an idea of earlier lifestyles. Here at West Kirkcarswell a low knoll preserves the remains of a near-circular stony rampart with a ditch outside. There is an entrance to the NW, but little remains to be seen inside the rampart.

Excavation on similar sites has shown that remains like this date from the Iron Age and relate to small defended farmsteads. The homestead at McNaughton's Fort in Dumfriesshire has been dated to the third century BC. Some sites are so small that they are likely to have contained no more than one timber house. Other, larger sites have been shown to contain clusters of buildings. Some may have housed several families, while others were home to a single, albeit extended, family with outhouses for stores and animals.

In many ways the daily routine of these Iron Age farmers had changed little from that of their Neolithic and Bronze Age ancestors. They still occasionally used flint blades, and fragments of coarse pottery have been found. Many of their belongings were made of organic materials such as wood, bone and antler. Iron tools were certainly known, and most households would have had at least one iron knife, but the coming of iron did not bring great changes to most people's lives. There were, however, other changes to society that clearly affected the lives of everyone. A deterioration in climate towards the end of the Bronze Age put pressure onto society as the upland livelihood of the hill farmers failed. Communities had to move downhill to survive and there was thus more competition for the land here. Fortified settlements became commonplace and the archaeological record indicates that a great number of weapons were in circulation. The introduction of iron working no doubt assisted the development of weaponry. The traditional emphasis on the community lessened and there was a rise in the importance of the individual. The scene was set for a warrior, tribal society.

The homestead of West Kirkcarswell is typical of its period. Stock had to be protected and houses could no longer sit, undefended, amongst the fields. The uncertainties of life, and one's neighbours, meant that attention was now paid to fortification. The low knoll must have provided an ideal site to place a small farmstead and fortify it against outsiders with the addition of a ditch and rampart.

Ven Law: settlement
Peeblesshire, NT 259 416
NT24SE 32

The grassy remains of a low circular bank may be seen in the foreground of **colour plate 4**. They comprise the vestiges of the boundary wall of a circular, scooped settlement, within which there are traces of some six round houses.

This settlement is typical of a type that was common in southern Scotland throughout later prehistory, some 2000 years ago. The inhabitants constructed an enclosing wall, which they faced with boulders to give it strength. It may well have been topped with brushwood, and would have served as much to keep local wild animals out as to keep their own animals in. Wolves and wild boar were still at large among the Scottish hills. The enclosure wall also acted as a boundary for those who lived there, and it could provide a statement to visitors of the local skills and wealth.

Inside, the enclosure was slightly scooped into the hillslope to provide a yard, and platforms were constructed to provide level foundations on which to build round houses. Traces of six platforms have been recorded here. Some of the houses no doubt provided family homes, but others served as byres or for storage. With time their uses no doubt shifted, as older houses fell into disrepair and new ones were built, just as any farming community today makes use of its space.

The settlement at Ven Law lies just above the upper limit of settlement today, and out of the normal range of modern farming. As the photo shows there is some pasture, but rough grassland and modern coniferous plantations dominate the present landscape. In the Iron Age, however, the scene was very different. The local hills are littered with traces of habitation from this time. There are other, similar, settlements and also several forts which suggest that life was not always peaceful and that neighbourly quarrels could sometimes get out of hand. It is unlikely that all of these sites were inhabited at the same time, but it is also important to remember that settlement extended down into the valleys, where better drained and cleared land could be made use of. There was clearly a substantial, if scattered, population here.

It is often hard to make sense of archaeological remains when seen at ground level. For this reason, archaeologists make great use of aerial photos, which can sometimes reveal more detail of a site and its setting. The aerial photo of Ven Law shows clearly the circular enclosing bank and the humps and bumps of the house platforms inside. The invasive furrows of modern forestry ploughing may also be seen around the site. Any traces of the prehistoric landscape which the inhabitants of Ven Law helped to shape have sadly been lost to modern progress.

See **colour plate 4**

Ardanaiseig: crannog
Argyll, NN 091 248
NN02SE 6

Crannogs are commonly defined as island-dwellings. They were to be found throughout much of prehistory and well into historical times, up to the seventeenth century, but they were most common in the Iron Age and early medieval periods. In some cases a crannog comprises an artificial island, built of stones, or with timbers, depending on the preferences of the locals and on the topography of the loch where they were building. Many crannogs, however, make use of natural features, such as small islets or rises in the loch-bottom which have been enhanced with stones and/or wood to provide a stable base for the dwelling.

Most crannogs would have supported only a single timber round house, probably with an outside walkway, though there are larger sites with space for more complex arrangements of buildings. Later crannogs sometimes have evidence for stone buildings and these are usually rectangular. Some crannogs are connected to land by a causeway: evidence of which may be seen running away to the right of the crannog in the photo. Other crannogs have evidence for small jetties. The remains of dug-out canoes have, not surprisingly, been found at many crannog sites.

The complex reasons why people built out in the water have been much studied. Defence has long been thought to be a prime concern for the lake-dwellers, but many other factors have to be taken into consideration. In some areas agricultural land was not readily available and by building their homes on islands the crannog-dwellers were able to maximise the space where they could grow crops and graze their livestock. This would be particularly important at a time of rising population, such as the Iron Age, when pressure on the land was increased by a worsening climate which forced many farmers to withdraw from the hills. In times such as these, local quarrels may well have added a defensive element to an otherwise peaceful choice of settlement. Other crannogs may have been bases for fishing and fowling, from which the usual supplies of a farming community could be augmented. In the later periods written sources relating to island building have survived and these show the great range of reasons behind these sites. There are references to islands used as dog kennels, others where kitchen ranges could be isolated away from a main settlement to minimize fire risk; some sites were important centres of local power; some were prisons, others great feasting-halls; and some may have provided way stations for travellers and drovers about to cross the loch.

Ardanaiseig is an unusually prominent site: it was capped with stones in the nineteenth century. It has never been subject to detailed excavation, though underwater survey has taken place here. Elsewhere, because of the preservation conditions associated with waterlogging, excavation on crannog sites has revealed rich detail of the life that went on there. Finds include fragments of cloth, wooden tools and structural elements, food remains (including a substance interpreted as butter), and even dung from the animals that were over-wintered in the dwelling along with their owners.

Achnahaird Sands: multi-period settlement and industrial remains
Ross and Cromarty, NC 016 131
NC01SW 2

Sand is a very mobile element and it has been known to blow over and cover areas of settlement and agriculture, even in relatively recent times. Likewise, sand can blow away, to reveal traces of past activity that were once hidden. The remains at Achnahaird suggest that people have lived here, on and off, from the late prehistoric period onwards.

The features at Achnahaird include the remains of structures as seen in the illustration, as well as shell heaps, charcoal patches, hearth sites, and spreads of artefact debris. The stone foundations of two sub-rectangular buildings have been recorded, the smaller of which has a rounded end. Indications of internal subdivisions survive, though one building has been altered by the insertion of a small rectangular pen in modern times. There are also remains of an enclosure, or yard, associated with the buildings, and short lengths of walling run away into the nearby dunes.

Visitors to the site have long collected objects from the surface of the dune blow-outs and archaeologists have tried to categorize these to make sense of the age and function of the site, but it is not easy. It would appear that human activity has taken place here for over three millennia and the artefacts found on the site are mixed from a variety of periods. The earliest material dates back some 4000 years and includes flint flakes and hammer stones which suggest that the prehistoric occupants of Achnahaird were making stone tools here. There is also coarse pottery that may date to this period, though no certain structural remains from this time have been found.

Most abundant at Achnahaird is metalworking debris, comprising mainly iron slag, with some copper alloy off-cuts, charcoal, and burnt stones. This activity has been dated by the discovery of a bronze ring brooch and a bronze pin, both of which would have been in use in the fourteenth century, though the pin may go back earlier. There would seem to have been considerable industrial activity here in the medieval and post-medieval period, and this is confirmed by the pottery fragments that have been collected. Other finds include the lower half of a rotary quern, and pieces of worked steatite. Excavations of part of the site showed that at least one of the buildings dates to the seventeenth century, and elsewhere nineteenth-century debris has been recorded. All in all, several episodes of use from prehistory until recent times have been documented.

As well as the structural remains and artefacts, the shell heaps suggest midden mounds, and these are associated with heaps of stones that may have resulted from clearance for agriculture. In addition, a square mound, capped with boulders has been recognised as a burial cairn. It is hard to make sense of what has been going on. Achnahaird is a complex site typical of the sort of remains that result from repeated, but changing, human use of the same well-favoured spot.

Pitcarmick Loch: sub-rectangular building
Tayside, NO 053 567
NO05NE 22

In the foreground of the picture a low, stony, wall-footing may be seen. This constitutes the remains of a long house with rounded ends. This house is one of a type of building that was only recognised in the late 1980s when the Royal Commission on the Ancient and Historical Monuments of Scotland undertook field survey in north-east Perthshire. It is a good example of how our understanding of the archaeological record is continually expanded.

Though the photograph shows a stretch of open heather moorland, it has not always been so. The archaeological remains show that at various periods this moorland has been home to a considerable population and that it was well cultivated. Prior to cultivation it is likely that areas like this were covered with an open, scrubby, woodland among which stands of larger trees thrived. The woodland, however, has long been under threat from the local population who needed to clear ground for farming and to gather timber for use as fuel, as well as for building and other purposes. The earliest cultivation and settlement remains here comprise extensive systems of small fields, associated with which there are groups of hut-circles and many clearance cairns (see p48). These date back well into prehistory. Set among them, and occasionally overlying them, are the foundations of the long Pitcarmick-type buildings that came into use later on.

Pitcarmick-type buildings comprise long, sub-rectangular buildings which tend to taper towards one of their rounded ends. They are often semi-sunken at the narrow end, where, perhaps, animals were byred. There is a single door towards the wider end in one of the long sides, usually with an outer porch for shelter and sometimes with the remains of a paved path running away from the house. These houses would have had low turf walls and thatched turf, or reed, roofs. They would seem to be associated with the remains of fields and cultivation, but it is difficult to distinguish these from the earlier, prehistoric cultivation remains associated with the hut-circles. In general, Pitcarmick-type buildings are thought to date to the early medieval period, and this was confirmed by excavation which yielded dates around the seventh century AD. It is likely, however, that houses like this one and its neighbours were occupied on and off over a long period, making use of the times when cultivation could expand out into the hill-lands.

The scene in the early-medieval period would thus have been a great contrast to the heather moorland of today. Ripening crops are attested by strips of rig and furrow, together with numerous clearance cairns, and livestock thrived. Low thatched houses dotted the landscape and all the noise of human settlement sounded where only grouse and other game birds are to be heard today. Children shrieked, dogs barked, messages were shouted above the low of the herd. This is likely to have been a brief respite, however. The archaeological indications do not suggest a long, well-established period of hill-settlement. As the climate closed down from time to time, so the farmers moved away to better lands and the heather moor took over once again, fossilizing the remains of their settlements and fields as the only indication that things were previously very different.

See **colour plate 5**

Dun Borrafiach: shieling mound
Skye, NG 236 633
NG26SW 2.04

In the Highlands of Scotland the medieval and later system of farming involved the transfer of cattle to summer pastures that were often on higher land. In this way the cattle could benefit from the rich high-level grassland, while allowing the recuperation of the lower pastures and protecting the ripening crops from their attention. It was the task of the women and children to accompany the herds up to the hills while their men-folk stayed in the settlement below. The group would stay away for several weeks at a time, and small clusters of huts, now known as shielings, were built to house the temporary community.

The shieling huts were simple dwellings, reflecting, perhaps, their temporary nature, and the weather conditions of the summer months. Most were built of turves or stones, depending on the local supplies. Some have ancillary cells and many sit on pronounced mounds where repeated repair and building work over the centuries have built up small 'tells' of archaeological material. Some stone shielings survive today almost to wall-head height (see p63), others are simply low mounds of grass. It is likely that the system was in use over many centuries, and so many different remains, dating from different periods, have built up across the land.

Many shieling groups are associated with patches of lush green pasture, and their Gaelic names can be very evocative: *the meadow of the five milk cows* is to be found on Rum. While they were away the families prepared cheeses and other foods for the winter months. This was a time for the repair of household items and for the telling of tales. Meanwhile, the men would labour on in the community below, tending to the crops and other repairs. There were also supplements to the food supplies to be taken in hand, such as fish. When autumn came and the weather closed in, the cattle would be taken down once again and the families joined together to work on the harvest and preparation of the grain.

The remains of shieling huts are dotted across Scotland in great profusion, a mute testimony to an order of things long gone. Here, by the Borrafiach Burn, the shieling huts sit well up above the level of cultivation today in a landscape that bears witness to considerable past activity. There are several groups of shieling huts, hut-circles with their associated cultivation remains from prehistoric times, and an Iron Age broch. We are constantly reminded that the landscape has not been static.

See **colour plate 6**

Linne a' Dhuais: deserted township
Argyll, NM 389 214
NM32SE 19

The changes in the landscape are not all ancient; many have taken place in relatively recent times. The ruins in the photograph reflect the fact that rural Scotland was once much more heavily populated than it is today. Throughout the Highlands and Islands of Scotland many of the tenant farmers were cleared from the land in the late eighteenth and nineteenth centuries as their landlords made way for new ventures such as sheep-farming. Prior to this, the rural population had greatly expanded, helped by the introduction of the potato, an exotic crop which thrived in the local conditions and offered an apparently stable food supply. The land could only support so many people, however, and so there were increasing pressures, compounded by the attitude of many landowners. There was little help for those who were moved off, or who found it just too hard to continue to eke a living.

In 1881 the settlement of Linne a' Dhuais was apparently still inhabited for it was recorded by the Ordnance Survey as a group of roofed buildings and a field. By 1960,

when this photo was taken, the roofs had long gone. The ruins are typical of those which dot the landscape as a reminder that the peaceful, wild-land scenery of today has not always been so. Here were once fertile fields and settled family homes.

Deserted townships are abundant across Scotland, and there is much variety in their appearance. At Harris on Rum (*NM 334 959; NM39NW 9*) a deserted settlement lies on a terrace overlooking the more recent township of Harris. The latter was abandoned in 1824, when the population emigrated to Canada at the behest of their landlord. The remains of the higher settlement are older but poorly preserved — they comprise low stony banks that mark out the house walls. In some cases they have been mutilated by later cultivation ridges that run across them. This not only provides evidence that the settlement on the terrace is earlier than that below, it is also an indication of need. It cannot have been easy for the inhabitants of the lower community to drive their cultivation across the stony remains of the houses of their predecessors. Perhaps by the early nineteenth century they were already feeling the pressures that came from too many mouths to feed.

Elsewhere the people did not always leave the lands of their ancestors straightway. In some cases they were offered other lands, albeit not the best. At Greod on the island of Sanday, just off Canna (*NG 247 045, NG20SE 24*), the grass-covered footings of several buildings have been recorded. These buildings lie close to the edge of an area of improved ground, and the settlement has been identified as that of a group of families who were moved here from Lag a' Bhaile on Canna. An estate map of 1805 shows a small settlement here, though by the late nineteenth century it was apparently abandoned. The first edition of the Ordnance Survey map of 1881 shows nothing at this spot.

See **colour plate 7**

Unish House: tacksman's house
Skye, NG 239 658
NG26NW 1.09

The upstanding remains of a substantial building in the landscape do not always indicate the historical interest that lies therein. Without an understanding of their past, it is all too easy to dismiss derelict buildings as visual debris.

Unish House appears to have been built in the late seventeenth or early eighteenth century as a two-storey house, with an entrance in the centre of the front wall looking out to sea and a central chimney stack. There were three rooms on each floor, with an attic, and the roof was thatched. After about 100 years the house was altered with the addition of a stair turret to the back wall, a wing was added to one end, and the windows were enlarged. The building seems to have been abandoned in the middle of the nineteenth century, but it was reoccupied and altered once more at the turn of the twentieth century. At this time the new wing was demolished, the gables were reduced and many windows blocked up, and the entrance was altered.

Unish House lies at the heart of a deserted township which is first documented in 1708, when a Donald Macleod took on the lease for 306 merks. This would tally nicely with the apparent date when Unish House was first built: Donald Macleod seems to have had some pretensions for his own home and for his newly acquired holdings. Macleod was a tacksman, he leased the estate, and sub-let tenancies for smaller farm holdings. In 1788 there was a total of 69 people living in the township: 10 married couples were recorded, together with 30 unmarried adults, 17 children and two widowed adults. The archaeological remains around Unish House include many cultivation remains as well as the traces of the houses of these families. There are sequences of lazy-beds from the tending of crops, small enclosures for stock and vegetables, and larger fields. None of the smaller houses has survived as well as Unish House: it was solidly built.

In 1796 the lands of Waternish were sold and Unish changed hands along with the rest of the land. It was perhaps at this time that the first alteration work on the house was started. In less than a hundred years, however, the thriving township was deserted and its population scattered. By 1880, when the surveyors from the Ordnance Survey visited, the main house was empty and only one house was occupied in the village. Unish House was briefly reoccupied at the turn of the century, when the final alterations took place. Since then the deserted remains and traces of cultivation here have stood as mute testimony to those who worked hard to make their living and raise their families.

See **colour plate 8**

3 FARMING AND OTHER LAND MANAGEMENT

A prime concern for the past population of Scotland has been the provision of food. In the first few millennia after the Ice Age this was fulfilled through the use of a natural harvest. Scotland is rich in resources and these could be taken in quantities sufficient to ensure adequate supplies in most years. Nuts, berries, tubers and wild grains could all be gathered, there was a range of mammals as well as birds to be hunted, and the resources of the rivers and seas — fish, shellfish, sea mammals, and birds — all added to the diet. It is likely that different elements provided nutrition at separate times of the year. The early inhabitants of Scotland developed a sophisticated knowledge of their land and how to get the most from it, and this was tied up with their mobile lifestyle.

About 5000 years ago a great change swept across Scotland with the introduction of a new way to get food: that of producing it yourself. The ideas behind this must have come in from the outside, along with some of the ingredients: sheep and certain grains for example were not native to Scotland. The existing intricate relationship between the local population and their environment meant that farming was quickly taken up in most areas, and communities soon came to rely on it. The adoption of farming was to have long term effects on the landscape as a whole suite of archaeological remains sprang up. Whereas earlier communities had taken what they needed without the construction of permanent monuments or changes to the landscape, the farming communities needed to alter the face of the land. Fields were cleared and boundaries built, a varied set of buildings served them and this developed with time as may be seen at Grumby.

The farmers did not, however, rely solely on the new ways. They continued to fish, hunt, and harvest the woodlands for nuts and berries. These old traditions have persevered down the millennia and still play their part today. Developments such as the use of stone fish traps (Loch a'Chumhainn) or the building of deer traps (Orval) have left their mark in the archaeological record and some of these may have very early foundations. Though food today is less and less a matter of home-production as we buy from industrial-scale enterprises, there is still an element of the past in all of us as we pick brambles, collect shellfish, or cut parsley from a pot on the windowsill.

In places the remains of the agricultural landscape are intense, as in the construction of cultivation terraces (Holyrood Park) to provide level ground for crops on a slope. In other places they are more gentle but widespread with different types of field remains (Croftmartaig or Canna). Generations of farmers have persevered to work the land — the repeated collection of stones and their deposition into stony clearance cairns to improve the soil for cultivation, show just how their efforts accumulate (Pitcarmick Burn). Other monuments provided for different needs: mills to provide power (Balmavicar); kilns to

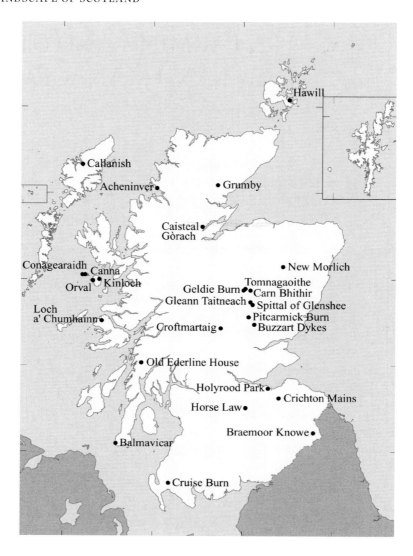

dry corn (Tomnagaoithe); and stills from which came illicit whisky (Carn Bhithir). The farming landscape of Scotland is a rich one.

But agriculture is not the only use of the land. Land management is a complex issue which draws together many elements. Industrial sites have been given their own chapter, but it can be hard to draw a dividing line, and of course the scale by which issues are judged changes with time. Much that appears small scale to us would, in the past have been considered quite industrial. The kelp burning that lead to numerous kiln remains (Conagearaidh) was quite an industry in the past. Other practices had a serious impact on the local population, while leaving little trace. The creation of deer parks, such as that at Buzzart Dikes in the fourteenth century, meant that normal farming practices had to be modified. Then, as now, the management of deer was a good example of how the domestic and wild characteristics of the landscape interact.

Finally, there are elements of land management that blur the division between the rural and urban landscapes, and gardens are a good example of this. Garden archaeology is a relatively recent specialisation. In Scotland it is given added interest by the abundance of policies — the domestic lands of an estate that were to be found round the big house. A policy might include several separate gardens, as well as other elements. The folly at Caisteal Gòrach is a good example of this, where the landowner deliberately altered the aspect of his policies to give a false sense of antiquity. At Kinloch, on Rum, similar processes took place and the policies included a variety of features designed to enhance the pleasure of guests to the island.

Pitcarmick Burn: stone clearance cairns
Perth and Kinross, NO 061 561
NO05NE 23

Across much of Scotland agriculture involved the laborious clearing of thousands of stones and boulders from the land in order to improve the soil and assist the tending of crops. These stones had to be put somewhere, and so heaps, known as clearance cairns, grew up. The photograph shows an area of moorland well above the limits of modern farms. There are, however, extensive traces of past cultivation, possibly from more than one period.

Most prominent in the photograph are the mounds from stone clearance. Clearance cairns abound across this landscape as witness to those who once worked to clear the stones and grow their crops between the mounds. Also visible are several hut-circles: two prominent circles lie to the lower right of the picture. These date from the later prehistoric period and they may well have been home to the farmers who first cleared the land. There are several field dykes, which may be associated with the cultivation, and there are also the remains of longer Pitcarmick-type buildings (see p38). These are likely to date to more recent times than the hut-circles, perhaps to the early medieval period, once round houses had gone out of fashion. One lies in the central foreground. After the Pitcarmick-type buildings came shieling huts, the summer houses of those who brought the cattle up to the richer, higher pastures. The shieling huts are harder to make out, though several appear.

This abundance of remains built up over a long period of time. The different features in the picture represent a series of layers that were separated, in this case, by periods of abandonment when the climate worsened and the farmers moved downhill. It is a complex picture, but a good example, nevertheless, of the detail that repays close study of the landscape. It is also a forceful reminder that the landscape which means so much to us today has not always been so. We are but another page in the book of the land.

From the ground these features can be much harder to distinguish. At Horse Law in Lanarkshire (*NT 031 504, NT05SW 17*) a spread of clearance cairns has been recorded and photographed (p49), but the low dark mounds of the cairns are not easy to make out under their heather capping. Once again these cairns lie above the limits of modern farming as a reminder that even apparently barren areas like this could once be cultivated. There are no clear house or hut sites at Horse Law, so it is impossible to date the cultivation, though it is likely that various turf and stone sheepfolds and other enclosures in the area are of recent date (within the last two centuries) and certainly much more recent than the clearance cairns.

Grumby: farmstead and stackyard
Sutherland, NC 712 091
NC70NW 133

See **colour plate 9**

The farmstead at Grumby was built in the nineteenth century and was abandoned just after the Second World War. It comprises a range of stone-built buildings, with a dwelling at their centre. These run along the southern side of a yard containing six stone stack stands. A byre stands to the west of the yard and there are various enclosures and animal pens as well as cultivation remains which surround the steading. Grumby was recorded as roofed when surveyed by the Ordnance Survey in 1879 and 1907.

Though it is not cultivated today, Grumby stands at the heart of a landscape which still bears the traces of countless generations of farmers who have built their houses and farmed there, on and off, over the millennia. The earliest remains in the vicinity comprise two hut-circles and a scatter of small clearance cairns from the late prehistoric period. Other, pre-nineteenth-century evidence includes the traces of various rectangular buildings with enclosures, fields and other cultivation remains.

The agricultural landscape around Grumby is a rich one, but it is hard to make out its detail from the ground. Aerial photography has played an important part in revealing the patterning left behind by past generations of farmers on the land. At Croftmartaig, Perthshire (*NN 750 433, NN74SE 24*) the traces of previous cultivation show up clearly from the air. The long lines of straight modern field walls cut across earlier walls and in some fields the ridges of ancient cultivation may be made out. There are the remains of long, thin rectangular buildings and other, more irregular, enclosures for livestock.

A very different sort of agriculture is to be seen from the air over Canna in the Small Isles (*NG244 056, NG20NW 131*). Here the short ridges of spade dug 'lazy-beds' combine to give a patchwork effect across the landscape. It is well over a hundred years since these landscapes have been farmed, but the land has held the evidence.

Spittal of Glenshee: cultivation remains
Perthshire, NO 108 703
NO17SW 6

Until recently, Glen Shee preserved a remarkable record of its past population in an extraordinary series of agricultural remains that extended along both sides of the valley. In contrast to the open nature of the land today, a number of settlements of differing sizes attested to the fertility of the land and the past presence of a rural community of considerable size. In addition, there were traces of earlier activity such as shieling sites as well as occasional prehistoric monuments. Glen Shee has been recorded as 'a remarkably intact pre-Improvement landscape' (RCAHMS 1990, 136). Sadly the traces of past cultivation here have fallen prey to the needs of the modern farming community. Recent ploughing has obscured many of the remains.

The photo shows one of the main areas of activity, that to the north-west of Spittal Church. On the terrace below the plantation lie the remains of a small fermtoun of some six units, each comprising a number of rectangular buildings clustered around a yard. Most survived only as grassy covered banks: humps and bumps that had to be interpreted by a trained eye to reveal their past history. Above the settlement ran the head-dyke which separated off the rough grazing land of the hill; on the slopes below and to the side lay the remains of a series of cultivation rigs. It is these ploughed ridges that stand out in this photo, taken during archaeological survey work in 1988. A hollow way ran across the slope on the uphill side of the head-dyke.

53

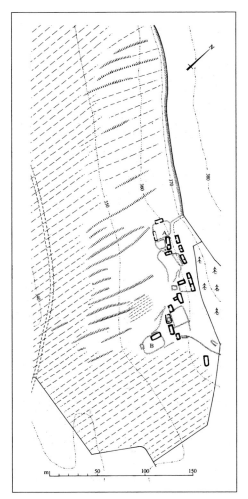

The site at Spittal was only one of a number of small settlements, which, together with their rigs, ran for over 2km along the valley sides. The past farming settlements of Glen Shee made use of the land at the margin of the cultivated ground but below the rough hill grazing. A well-built head-dyke served to keep the stock from the crops. Study of these remains has been amplified by historical reference which helps to people the valley for there are many early documentary references to the glen and her population. The process by which the land was brought into cultivation and 'improved' from the sixteenth century onwards, often displacing the traditional shieling grounds, is well recorded, especially in the eighteenth and nineteenth centuries. The community at Spittal itself, however, does not appear in the records, though it is likely to have been a site of some importance, in close relation to the church and mill. It is possible that it represented an earlier, medieval, phase of cultivation. Whatever its date, the settlement had apparently gone out of use and been forgotten by 1808, when Brown surveyed the land for the Invercauld Estates, of which it was a part. He annotated the site simply as 'Old House Lets' (RCAHMS 1990, 138).

Braemoor Knowe: cultivation terraces
Roxburghshire, NT 785 219
NT72SE 17

Past systems of agriculture have all left their traces in the ground, often as systems of long banks known as rigs. These may result from both hand-dug spade cultivation and from ploughing, where soil is continually up-cast into the centre of a rig, both to provide good soil for the crops and to assist drainage in the furrows that developed in between. Rigs tend to occur on flatter ground, or in areas of gentle slope only. Areas with a steeper topography called for a slightly different approach from the farmer.

Cultivation terraces developed when the steeper areas were prepared for crops. In some cases the rigs could run with the contour, instead of across it, resulting in a series of flat topped 'steps' up the hill along which crops could be grown. Where the land sloped more steeply, however, deliberate terraces had to be cut. Stones were cast aside into the terrace front and served to bank it up, and the flat terrace surface provided a suitable space to be ploughed. In practice it is hard to distinguish between horizontal rigs and terraces. However they were formed, the end result was much the same: a series of broad terraces that would once have borne ripening grain.

Terraces were once much more common across Scotland. Many have been obliterated by more recent agriculture. At Braemore Knowe a group of terraces extends up the hillside as a reminder that cultivation once extended into areas rarely touched today.

Though they are an important feature of the rural landscape, cultivation terraces may also occur in surprising places. Holyrood Park, right at the heart of the City of Edinburgh, is a remarkable piece of fossilized agricultural countryside, and amongst its many remains is the series of cultivation terraces that overlook Dunsapie Loch (*NT 279 729, NT27SE 76*). Holyrood Park bears extensive traces of past farming, often, as is the case here, making use of the more gently sloping and warmer east-facing ground where fertile soils built up during the last glaciation. These terraces are associated with rigs on the more gently sloping land below, and they were last tilled in 1616, though they may go back well before that. These are some of the best-preserved cultivation terraces in Scotland and they act as a timely reminder that even at the heart of the city all has not always been the same.

See **colour plate 10**

Tomnagaoithe: kiln barn
Aberdeenshire, NO 027 892
NO08NW 7

A corn kiln was an integral and important part of most eighteenth- and early nineteenth-century farming communities. With an uncertain climate such as that of Scotland it was important to be able to dry the corn thoroughly in order to store and process it.

The settlement at Tomnagoithe comprises at least nine ruinous buildings together with extensive cultivation remains, including spreads of rig and furrow and several stone clearance heaps. The kiln barn was built to one end of the group of buildings. The structure of the kiln itself is relatively well preserved and comprises a circular bowl nearly 2m deep. This seems to have been dug into the natural slope of the land: it is stone lined inside, but turf-backed on the outside. The flue runs below the bowl, and opened into the barn which is a stone building tacked on to the kiln.

A detailed study of the ruins at Tomnagoithe has suggested that there were various periods of alteration within the life of the settlement. This would only be natural, but it is often hard to separate out the details within any one site. Here, the ruins of at least one longhouse are overlain by stone clearance heaps. Cultivation obviously took place in the vicinity of this house once it had fallen out of use and well into decay. Several buildings show signs of internal alteration and phasing, and finally, two other buildings are of notably better construction than the others. These, perhaps, represent the last phase of building in the township, when squared corners and more regular coursed masonry were in common use.

Tomnagoithe today appears relatively barren, though it was not always so. Prior to the farming communities of recent centuries there would have been more open woodland here, though this was threatened even by the first hunters who roamed these hills some 10,000 years ago. Around 6000 years ago the first farmers cleared the trees to make space for their crops and their cattle, but even after they left the land would never be the same again. Farmers came and went, depending on the vagaries of the climate and social pressures. Today, the colours of the land show up the once fertile ground as green pasture which holds its own against the purple heather of the surrounding moorland.

See **colour plate 11**

Geldie Burn: sheep dip
Aberdeenshire, NO 009 872
NO08NW 20

Life for the rural communities of Scotland has always involved many different activities which have left varying traces in the landscape. It is often hard for the archaeologist to distinguish the 'signature' of a specific activity and separate it out from the rest. In many cases local knowledge helps to fill out the archaeologist's interpretation of an area, and this is what has happened here.

The remains in the illustration lie among a group of ruins which include six huts and various stock enclosures and pens. They comprise a low ramp from which run two rows of boulders. The latter probably provided the supports for a timber passageway. This leads to a pit, within which the sheep were dipped, and there is a cobbled drying stance to one side.

The sheep dip is relatively recent in date, but it is an important part of the historical record that has been set into the landscape. Though the face of the countryside changed with the clearance of the rural farming population and the introduction, in many areas, of sheep, this did not mean that human activity here had ceased. The sheep still had to be cared for and the land had to be managed. This, in turn, bought its own suite of archaeological remains. The bothies of the mountain shepherds, in various states of repair, dot many highland estates, together with stock enclosures, stells and other remains. Today, land use has changed once again, and it is still changing. Everything that we do adds another layer to the face of the hills. The close-packed plantation of conifers in the picture itself represents a trend in land use that will leave its own suite of remains and provides a contrast to the days when sheep dominated the landscape here. Even now that trend is moving on and different activities — recreation, conservation and others — are continuing to change the face of the land.

Balmavicar: horizontal mill
Argyll, NR 593 097
NR50NE 1

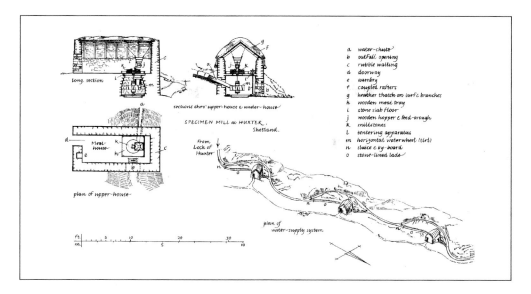

a   water-chute
b   outfall opening
c   rubble walling
d   doorway
e   aumbry
f   coupled rafters
g   heather thatch on turf & branches
h   wooden meal tray
i   stone slab floor
j   wooden hopper & feed-trough
k   millstones
l   tentering apparatus
m   horizontal waterwheel (tirl)
n   sluice & by-board
o   stone-lined lade

The deserted township of Balmavicar lies on the southernmost point of Kintyre, just to the north of the Mull lighthouse. It was recorded as uninhabited in a census of the Argyll Estates in 1779, though there are several earlier references to it and to the McVicar family who lived there in the seventeenth century. The township comprises the remains of several stone-built houses and byres, together with their enclosures, cultivation systems, and clearance heaps. It occupies the sloping land that runs westwards down to the sea, terminating in a cliff some 20m above the shore. The coastline is rocky and has no sign of safe landing places, though it would have been possible to fish from the rocks.

Rural communities like this had to be pretty self sufficient, and Balmavicar was no exception. The ruins include a kiln-house to dry the corn after harvest, and a small mill to grind the grain into flour, shown here. The mill stands on the banks of the Balmavicar Burn, which runs through the settlement. There are traces of a dam and a small lade to control the water supply. The mill house originally comprised two, stone-built, storeys, though the upper storey has almost gone. It was a horizontal water-mill, otherwise known as a 'click-mill', and there would have been a small wooden wheel which lay horizontally in the lower chamber which lies at the centre of the photo. As water was directed across the wheel from the lade, it turned the millstone in the chamber above, and here there was a small wooden clapper fixed to the upper stone. With each revolution of the stone this knocked against the grain hopper to shake out the grain. It made a rhythmic clicking noise as it did so, hence the name for this type of mill. The timber components of the Balmavicar mill have long gone and no signs of the mill stones remain. The reconstruction drawings of the mills at Huxter in Shetland give a good idea of the workings of a click mill.

Mills such as this have been shown to go back into Norse times. They were fairly easy to build and required minimal water supply and maintenance. Though they would never turn great wheels or provide much power, they were ideally suited to the needs of a small community and so were common throughout Scotland, though there are few extant today.

Carn Bhithir: illicit whisky still
Aberdeenshire, NO 081 876
NO08NE 19

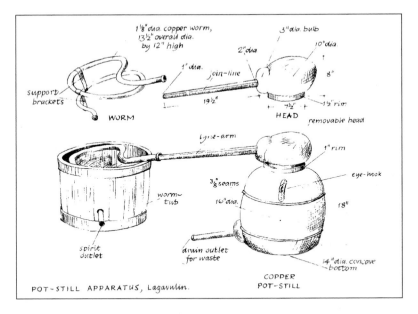

POT-STILL APPARATUS, Lagavulin.

The requirements of a rural community clearly included a 'drop of the hard stuff', especially for the cold winter nights or times when the harvest had not been so good. Originally, whisky could be made privately and most communities indulged in this. After the introduction of taxation and legislation in the eighteenth century, however, the distillation of illegal alcohol became a more precarious occupation, though it was still common well into the nineteenth century when the controls became more effective.

The remains of small whisky stills are intentionally difficult to find. Not only were they often set in hidden locations, but also they may contain little to physically connect them to distilling (for one good reason: they were designed to be dismantled and disguised quickly). The structure here is set within a group of shielings, the dwellings of those who looked after the cattle while they grazed on the summer pastures. There was quite a community here and it is not surprising to find that people occupied themselves with other tasks to prepare for the winter months ahead while keeping an eye on the herds.

The remains comprise a small, stone-built hut, set in a gully at the back of a terrace and hidden by a knoll from the valley below. Traces of a lade run up to an opening at one end of the hut. Water was necessary, both to steep the barley prior to distillation, and for the distillation process itself. There is no trace of the actual distilling equipment which was often very simple and designed to be easily, and quickly, dismantled and concealed. Drawings of equipment from Lagavulin, Islay, give an idea of the type of pot still that could be used.

See **colour plate 12**

Gleann Taitneach: shieling-huts
Perthshire, NO 082 737
NO07SE 24

Gleann Taitneach is a deep upland glen with a broad floor, along which winds the Allt Ghlinn Taitneach. The southern end of the glen runs into Glen Shee and here farmsteads and shieling sites abound, together with cultivation remains which contrast greatly with the abandoned and apparently barren nature of the land today. The northern part of the glen is more stony, but there are still tracts of rough pasture and grassy terraces that were sought out in the past. Here, on a terrace high on the valley sides, an area of rough pasture has provided summer grazing for the cattle when they were brought up into the shieling pastures from the settlements further down the valley.

The herders who bought their animals here needed shelter throughout the summer months and so they built two stone buildings, clear traces of which survive today. The buildings are both round-ended and divided into two compartments by a partition wall

which may have served as a central pillar to support the roof. There are also two stock enclosures, one of which has been subdivided into two. The remains of a small turf hut not far away may have been associated with the settlement.

This is just one of many shieling sites in Glen Taitneach. It is unlikely that all were in occupation simultaneously, but the valley obviously provided rich sheiling pastures close to necessary sources of fresh water. The huts would have been in occupation throughout the summer months when the cattle were brought up the valleys, traditionally by the women and children. Most shieling huts are simple single compartment dwellings, and there is some evidence in contemporary writings that more elaborate structures such as those in the photo may have belonged to more affluent families (RCAHMS 1990, 12). Many huts had small chambers where milk and dairy produce could be stored. An important part of the routine during the shieling period would be the preparation of cheeses for the winter months.

By the late nineteenth century the shieling system had all but died out, and in 1867 these huts in Glen Taitneach were depicted as unroofed by the Ordnance Survey surveyors.

Callanish: peat cuttings and antiquarian diggings
Western Isles, Lewis, NB 213 330
NB23SW 1

The grand stone setting of Callanish (Callanais) stands proud today in an area of low-lying peat. But it was not always so. When Callanais was built, some 5000 years ago, the ground level lay roughly where it lies today and the thick, black blanket of peat had not yet begun to form and hide the land. Soon after, however, the climate declined and a long wet spell ensued. One result of this was the growth of blanket bog, and the land surface gradually disappeared under a cover of peat. By the mid-nineteenth century only the tops of the stones were visible.

Peat, however, was a valuable commodity, used as fuel throughout the Highlands and Islands, where timber was scarce and other fuels expensive. Individual families each had rights to an area of peat moorland where they worked hard through the early summer, before the harvest started, in order to cut and dry the peaty turves that they would need as fuel throughout the winter. The traces of these peat cuttings may still be seen to surround the site.

In the nineteenth century, antiquarian interest in the site was increasing and, in 1857, the owner of the land, Sir James Matheson, arranged for the peat to be cut from around the buried stones so that they might be better seen. The work was carried out in October of that year, and the workmen cut away some 5ft of peat before they came to a rough stony layer that seemed to coincide with the original ground surface of the stones. As they worked they also uncovered the remains of a cairn with a small central chamber at the heart of the main setting. This was all carefully planned and a talk on the work was given to the Society of Antiquaries of Scotland in Edinburgh in the following year.

Matheson arranged for some re-erection and repair to be done to the setting, and a cobbled access path to the site was erected from the village nearby. Since then Callanais has attracted many visitors, all interested in the antiquity and purpose of the stones, but only in recent years has more work been done to help understand the monument and interpret it for its visitors. Callanais today still sits in a slightly dished setting, where the peat was cut away over 100 years ago.

In the photograph various houses can also be seen. People have always lived around the monument. In the lower right-hand corner of the photo lie the traces of a long-abandoned farm, and a drawing made in the mid-nineteenth century show just how close to the stones some of these habitations were. Excavations of a similar site at The Stones of Stenness in Orkney have yielded traces of a Neolithic settlement that thrived close by the monument some 5000 years ago: the tradition of dwelling in the vicinity of powerful stone settings may be an old one.

See **colour plate 13**

Cruise Burn: burnt mound
Dumfries and Galloway, NX 179 634
NX16SE 88

A low mound may be seen in front of the wall in this photo. This is the remains of a burnt mound which measures over 7m across. As the name implies, burnt mounds are comprised largely of burnt stones together with charcoal. This is seen more clearly in the section where the mound material has been cut through and its make-up exposed. Burnt mounds were in use throughout the later part of prehistory from the Bronze Age into the Iron Age and beyond.

Burnt mounds are common features of the Scottish landscape, and archaeologists have suggested various functions for them. Most seem to have served as communal cooking places; they may well have been associated with feasting and ceremonial rituals, as well as on more mundane occasions. There are accounts from early Irish tradition that tell of great communal hunts and the subsequent feasts where the meat was cooked at an open site. Other possible functions include use as saunas or sweat lodges. Whatever their use, most burnt mounds contain abundant evidence of fire and heating: rounded stones are thought to have been heated on the hearth and then dropped into a water-filled tank to heat the water. The sweepings from the hearth and other rubbish, including any shattered stone debris, were periodically cleared to one side where, over time, they built up into the characteristic mound.

Most burnt mounds are situated close to running water. Water was clearly essential to the activities that took place therein and cooking would be quite in keeping with this. The centre of the mound at Cruise Burn has a marked hollow some 2m across that opens out towards the stream that runs to one side. Similar hollows are found on many burnt mounds and they normally contain traces of a sub-rectangular pit. Elsewhere, in the Northern Isles, as at Hawill in Orkney (*HY 512 065, HY50NW 10*), the burnt mounds often contain traces of stone-built structures. These may contain rectangular troughs as well as hearth sites, together with roughly built wind-breaks which hold back the burnt debris. The abundance of slab-like stones and the lack of wood in Orkney may have given rise to this geographical distinction.

Crichton Mains: souterrain
Midlothian, NT 400 619
NT46SW 11

Souterrains are subterranean structures, so there is generally little to be seen on the ground surface except where a structure has collapsed. At Crichton in Midlothian a small 'creep' gives access into a well-preserved souterrain that was re-roofed in the nineteenth century. The souterrain here comprises a long curving passage some 15m in length and 2m wide, with a side passage. Most souterrains are simple in plan, though some have side passages and others, especially in the Northern Isles, terminate in small round chambers.

Souterrains mostly date from the late prehistoric period, some 2000 years ago. They are usually associated with settlement, and often lead out of round houses. Most seem to have been used for storage, and archaeologists are divided as to whether their hidden nature was an important part of the design. Restricting access to one's private stores may well have been a wise decision, even in times of relative peace. Little cultural material has ever been found in souterrains; some may have been carefully cleared out before abandonment, but it is also likely that most of the goods stored were organic (foodstuffs, clothes, objects of wood), and so have long since decayed.

The souterrain at Crichton is interesting because the masonry of which it was built incorporates dressed blocks that have apparently been taken from a Roman building. Some of these blocks can be seen in the upper courses, on the right-hand side of the passage in the photo. In addition to the dressed blocks, one of the lintels of the souterrain has a small carving of a Pegasus. The winged horse, Pegasus, was the emblem of one of the Roman Legions: the Legio II Augusta. They would have been active in the area, and it is likely that the native builders of the souterrain took some of their masonry from a nearby military post. This also helps to date the building of the souterrain to some time in the Antonine period in the second century AD.

Today souterrains show up mainly in aerial photographs as crop marks in cultivated fields, where the differentiation between the crops growing over the passage makes a characteristic banana-shaped blotch in the field. On occasion, one may be found when a tractor, or other heavy machinery, cracks a roof slab and drops into the void below. In the past, many souterrains have been uncovered during the course of farming and subsequently filled in and lost. At New Morlich, Aberdeenshire (*NJ 444 147, NJ41SW 1*) the entrance to a souterrain was clearly visible in the latter part of the nineteenth century, and into the early twentieth century. It is reported to have collapsed around 1915 and been filled with rubble. The photo was taken in the 1930s at which point most of the structure had been blocked off. By 1998 the site had been covered with earth and nothing was visible.

Acheninver: mill
Ross and Cromarty, NC 041 055
NC00NW 23

The remains of a small, over-shot mill lie towards the mouth of the Allt Ach a' Bhraighe at Acheninver. This comprised a small stone-built rectangular building, to one side of which was a wheel pit, about 1m wide. The groove for the axle of the wheel can still be clearly seen. The remains of an embanked lade run up to the edge of the wheel pit, and there are traces that may be the remains of a dam some 15m away to the north. An undressed millstone lies within the ruins of the mill.

This was a larger mill than that at Balmavicar (pp60-1) and it is a reminder of the different needs of individual communities across Scotland. Overshot mills were more efficient than the horizontal mills and so the community could take in more grain, perhaps from further afield. Rural communities were largely self-sufficient and the mill was an important feature of rural life. The mill at Acheninver lies amidst a group of structural remains including two possible long houses and various enclosures. In 1881 it was depicted on the Ordnance Survey map (Cromartyshire 1881, sheet vii) as a rectangular building with an enclosed garden (traces of which may still be seen today). By 1906, when the Ordnance surveyors visited once again, it had been abandoned.

Buzzart Dikes: deer park
Perthshire, NO 126 476
NO14NW 2

Farming has always been only one of many interests in the land, and successive management regimes over the centuries have had to juggle various interests and their different needs. In north-east Perth the Royal Forest of Clunie saw increased pressure from both encroaching settlement and other activities throughout the fourteenth and fifteenth centuries. One result of this was the establishment of two deer parks which could be managed exclusively for hunting. One, Laighwood, was created out of land granted to the Earl of Moray by Robert II in the late fourteenth century. The other, Buzzart Dikes, seen here, is not documented, but seems to date to the same period.

The park at Buzzart Dikes was enclosed by an earthwork, or pale, traces of which survive round all but the east side, across the lower foreground in the photograph. There was a ditch on the inside of the bank and an area of some 86ha was enclosed. The remains of two stone-built buildings lie just inside the park on its northern side, and traces of a further large rectangular building lie some 300m to the north. These may have been associated with the park.

In common with many ancient remains, Buzzart Dikes was long thought to be the traces of a 'Caledonian Camp' associated with the battle of Mons Graupius at which the Romans defeated the Caledonian forces in AD 83. It was only in the late 1940s that archaeological fieldwork, associated with aerial survey, identified it as the remains of a medieval deer park.

See **colour plate 14**

Orval: deer trap
Rum, NM 329 986
NM39NW 56

Rum is a National Nature Reserve, well known for the herds of red deer that graze across the island. Today the deer are regarded as an important part of the natural interest of the island. Deer are managed as an integral part of the island wildlife and their lifestyle has been part of a long and detailed study. In the past, however, they formed part of the natural assets of Rum that contributed to its value as a sporting estate. Rum venison has long been prized, and through the nineteenth century successive landowners introduced new breeding stock to try to maintain and improve the quality of the herd. At that time there was only a small human population on the island which was managed largely as a playground for the rich.

Prior to the nineteenth century the deer were an important asset for the people of Rum who, by the late eighteenth century, had come to number well over 400. Life on Rum was tough for its inhabitants for there was barely enough fertile ground to support a population of this size. It was at this time that the potato came into its own, together with oats and bere barley, as a basic staple of the diet which was supplemented with fish, dairy produce and small quantities of meat. The inhabitants of Rum kept cattle, sheep and goats. Meat from the red deer provided a welcome addition to the diet.

In contrast to the later sporting hunters of the nineteenth and more recent centuries, the inhabitants of Rum worked together to hunt deer. High on the slopes of Orval they constructed two low walls which lead downhill into a small corral. Some members of the community set out to frighten the deer who then took to the hills from whence there was no escape except down into the funnel. This channeled them down into the corral, from where they could easily be killed by others who lay in wait for them. This was very much a communal hunt, a way to maximise the meat obtained for everyone.

Traces of traps such as that on Rum have been discovered in various parts of the world where they were well known, going far back into prehistory. There are several traps on Rum, all in the area around Orval and Ard Nev, but so far none have been discovered (or recognised) elsewhere in Scotland. This was, however, a common way to hunt deer in historic times and several contemporary Scottish accounts of hunts such as this exist (Love 1983; Magnusson 1997). The efficacy of the 'tainchell' (or tinchel) hunt, as it was known, may be judged by the fact that by the 1780s all red deer on Rum had been exterminated. This no doubt contributed to the 'air of famine' recorded by many visitors to the island (Love 1983), and in the 1820s the local population left to make a new life in Nova Scotia while the landowner turned the island over to sheep farming.

See colour plates 15 & 16

Loch a' Chumhainn: fish trap
Mull, NM 428 516
NM45SW 20

Throughout history the average diet of a farming community has always been supplemented one way and another. The skills of hunting, gathering and fishing did not die out with the introduction of farming some 5000 years ago. While access to some resources, such as deer herds, could be strictly controlled, sea fish were more easily harvested. In many places stone traps were built to allow fish to pass at high tide, but trap them as the tide receded, thus allowing the local community to wade in and collect them. In contrast to the solitary sport fishers of today, many fish traps played a more communal role.

The fish trap in the photo is particularly well preserved. It comprises a stone wall across the narrow sea loch, Loch a' Chumhainn, in western Mull and runs from the settlement of Dervaig across to a small tidal island, Eilean na Carraidh. The wall is not straight, but incorporates two deeply indented 'v'-shaped inlets, each about 8m deep. These, apparently, assisted the ingress of fish. It is likely that the stone base of the trap supported a wattle or hurdle superstructure which has subsequently decayed. Stake nets were probably set at the base of each inlet, into which the fish would be funneled. Traps like this would serve well to catch estuarine species, such as plaice and flounder, as well as eels and other visiting migratory fish, such as salmon and sea trout.

There are many remains of fish traps around Scotland, but this one is in a particularly good state of repair. In some places the wall stands as much as 1.8m high. The archaeological records note that it has been maintained over the centuries by successive generations of one local family. The upper levels of the wall, therefore, are relatively recent and comprise small boulders that can be easily replaced. The lower levels, however, are built of much more massive boulders and over time the wall has attained a width of nearly 2m. There are no records of the early use of fish traps such as these, but it is likely that they are of considerable antiquity. There is no reason why some structures such as this should not reach back into prehistory.

Appropriately, the neck of land from which the trap is built is known as Druim na Carraidh, and it runs out to an island known as Eilean na Carraidh. The element 'Carraidh' in these names has been identified as a variant of 'cairidh', which is the Gaelic for a fish trap.

Conagearaidh: kelp kiln
Canna, NG 214 057
NG20NW 28

The traces of the small, rectangular, stone structure seen in **colour plate 17** are typical of many set around the coasts of Scotland, particularly in the Western and Northern Isles. They relate to the burning of kelp — locally gathered seaweed — the calcined ashes of which were an important source of alkali. The alkali was used further south in the industrial heartlands of Britain, in industries such as glass and soap-making.

Seaweed had long been important to the local farmers who spread it as fertiliser over their lands. The kelp industry gave it an added value. The industry flourished throughout the eighteenth, and start of the nineteenth, century, when other forms of alkali were expensive and hard to get as a result of the American Wars of Independence and the Napoleonic Wars. Though it was not industry on a grand scale, the kelp-burning did bring a very different atmosphere (literally) to the islands during the seasons of work. Contemporary accounts speak of the palls of smoke that hung over the islands for days at a time, as seen in this photo taken at Kenavara on Tiree at the turn of the twentieth century. Between 1764 and 1772 nearly 5000 tons of kelp were processed annually in Scotland, and most of this came from the Western and Northern Isles.

Work on the kelp industry was seasonal, but it was very labour intensive. The seaweed had to be harvested and laid out to dry, the kilns had to be tended, and the glassy slag that resulted when it was burnt had to be taken to the boats and loaded for export. The industry brought changing economic values to the land, as formerly 'un-interesting' areas acquired a value. Most of the profit went to the landowners who controlled the industry; to them it brought great wealth, and a number of elegant houses date from this period. Some profit did percolate down to the workers, however: small luxuries like tea and imported clothes could be bought. But it also meant that many island populations remained high, as people were not tempted to seek work elsewhere. When the industry declined in the early nineteenth century, due to easier access to cheaper sources of alkali, the loss of work could only add to the general sorrows of the time.

See **colour plate 17**

Old Ederline House: ice house
Argyll, NM 870 029
NM80SE 79.03

Throughout the nineteenth century ice was a precious commodity, important for the preservation of food both before and after preparation, as well as for the preparation of ice creams and sorbets during the summer. An ice house was an essential part of the estate buildings from the late eighteenth century onwards, and most large estates had at least one pond from which thick blocks of ice could be cut in the winter and taken to the ice house by horse and cart or sled.

Ice houses were carefully built to maintain low temperatures and preserve their contents. They were often semi-subterranean with thick walls, small entrances, and drainage holes through which the melting water could be channelled away. The advent of refrigeration in the late nineteenth century meant that they were no longer needed and they gradually fell into disuse as the kitchens of the great houses were fitted with this latest invention.

This is an unusual ice house: it is a domed, circular building with rubble walls. There is a low entrance passage. Like most ice houses it has been allowed to fall into disrepair and nature has started to reclaim it into the landscape. Abandoned ice houses are a common feature of the countryside. Today, most blend well into the landscape, but they are to be found wherever there has once been an old estate. Ice houses were also built in the towns: ice was just as important to the wealthy citizens of Edinburgh or Glasgow, for example, though they usually had to buy it commercially from ice merchants who cut the blocks from local ponds or lochans. Within the city today few ice houses survive; some have been long since converted into other uses, for example in the mews of

Edinburgh's New Town, but the sites of most old ice houses were quickly redeveloped once they were no longer needed.

Ice was also needed for industrial purposes, especially related to the preservation of fish as the herring industry developed in the nineteenth century. Ice houses are therefore an integral part of the remains of the herring and salmon stations around the coasts of northern Scotland. Most of these are built on a much larger scale than the domestic ice houses though the basic principals were the same. Many of the commercial ice houses survive; some have been converted into different uses while others have fallen into disrepair.

Caisteal Gòrach: folly
Ross and Cromarty, NH 544 611
NH56SW 38

The ruins of Caisteal Gòrach stand impressively on Tulloch Hill, near Dingwall. But from close to, it is obvious that all is not as it should be. A hint as to the origins of these remains is given in their name. Caisteal Gòrach translates as 'Silly Castle', and that, roughly, is what it is. It was built as a ready-made ruin, a folly, for Duncan Davidson, the owner of nearby Tulloch Castle. In the landscape, nothing is ever what it seems.

Caisteal Gòrach was built in the late eighteenth century at a time when respectable landowners felt that they needed some ruins to lend an air of ancestral interest to their estates. Davidson took his idea very seriously and contracted the famous architect Robert Adam to design and build it. Copies of Adam's original sketches survive in the National Monuments Record of Scotland. Adam packed all the well-known qualities of a ruined castle into his building. It had a round tower, flanking walls that led to mock square towers on each side, arrow slits, a round-headed doorway, and a ruined window opening above. There were even picturesque, stunted pine trees growing out of the ruined battlements. From behind it was obvious that it had never been intentioned to function as a building. The ruins were built as a screen on Tulloch Hill, to catch the eye and attract the curiosity of Davidson's guests as he took them round his estate. Caisteal Gòrach would have provided a romantic backdrop for their picnics.

Kinloch: castle policies
Rum, NM 403 995
NM49NW 12

Throughout the nineteenth century many landowners built grand new houses for themselves. Advances in technology meant that these could now be equipped with many comforts and luxuries that were previously unthought of. This practice extended to their policies: the surrounding gardens; plantations; and home farm. Kinloch Castle on Rum is a good example of this. It was built at the end of the nineteenth century, and the landowner, George Bullough, son of wealthy industrial magnates from Lancashire, spared no expense.

Kinloch Castle itself is quite magnificent, but no less interesting is the landscape immediately surrounding it. Soil was brought by boat from Ayrshire to improve the marshy ground where the castle was built, and splendid gardens were laid out. These included a Japanese garden with stylish wrought-iron bridges, fine grassy lawns, a bowling green, a nine hole golf course, turtle ponds, a large walled garden, and conservatories with peaches and palms, as well as avenues, rose gardens and riverside walks. The grounds were well stocked. Trees were planted, plants brought in, and 12 gardeners worked full time to look after their well-being. Although the Bulloughs only visited Rum for a few months in the year, the design and upkeep of their grounds were obviously important to them.

Alas, the grandeur of Kinloch Castle lasted only a short time. After the First World War, society's enjoyment of this opulent lifestyle began to decline. The Bulloughs' visits to Rum became more and more infrequent. The gardens fell into decay as the heating systems broke down and weeds infested the flowerbeds. George Bullough died in 1939 and he is buried at Harris on the south-west coast of Rum, in a Grecian-style mausoleum. After his death, Lady Bullough rarely visited the island, and in 1957 she sold it to the Nature Conservancy Council, in whose care it rests (NCC is now known as Scottish Natural Heritage).

Rum is now a National Nature Reserve; people arrive from all round the world to look at the rocks, flora and fauna. But around the castle, the traces of the old policies survive: a fascinating, overgrown and derelict glimpse into a world long forgotten. Carved stone benches hide under the undergrowth, elaborately wrought gates and ornamental bridges lead nowhere, roses have turned to briars, bamboos grown into thickets, and rhododendrons rampage away from the trees. The past glories of Rum have left their mark on the land.

See **colour plate 18**

4 FORTIFICATION IN THE LANDSCAPE

It is easy to give the impression that life in the past was idyllic, but of course this was not so. Neither was it always bleak or depressing. From relatively early on there are indications of pressures, and one thing that stands out is the rise in importance of remains that include elements of defence and aggression — fortifications. This is first clearly visible in the Iron Age, the period first illustrated here. There are earlier signs, but they are harder to make out: skeletons with wounds from weaponry; the weaponry itself; forts with early foundations that only appear through archaeological excavation.

Though they are not the earliest fortified sites, brochs have been chosen to head this chapter as they provide some of the most spectacular remains and they are peculiarly Scottish (Infield and Mousa). Even today archaeologists cannot agree on the interpretation of the abundant broch sites in the Scottish landscape. Did they all reach three or more storeys? Were they all defensive? Why do some not have a secure water supply? Were they permanently inhabited? What was their role in the complex society of the day? Brochs remain some of the most mysterious sites of the Scottish past.

Numerous other fortified sites abound in the Iron Age. There are forts of various sizes (Fallburn, Cademuir), small duns (Dunan nan Nighean), and crannogs (Loch an Duin on Taransay). Together they emphasise an important characteristic of the Scottish landscape. The topography of Scotland has lent itself to fortification and it is hard not to get the impression that a concern with personal security affected everyone.

Whatever the nature of life in the Iron Age, 2000 years ago there were new, and good, reasons to be worried: Romans! The incursion of foreign invaders with very different ways to those of the locals of southern Scotland must have been seen as a threat. This is clear from the archaeological record, and the fortified settlements came into their own. Things did not always go as the Romans wished, and this is shown by the abundant remains of Roman fortifications as the Roman army advanced and retreated on repeated occasions, struggling to maintain control over these northern frontier-lands of their Empire (Ardoch and Rough Castle). Their impact was only temporary, however, and after some 200 years they left.

The going of the Romans did not signal a return to more peaceful conditions. Continued inter-tribal fighting, and repeated threats from the outside, meant that fortification remained an important element of domestic settlement. Documentary sources and artefact research show that in the centuries immediately after the Romans there were broad regroupings of the peoples of Scotland.

In the Highlands this was the time of the Pictish Kingdoms. Pictish art suggests the importance and skills of their warriors. The Picts were known for the strength of their navy, and relations with their neighbours were fragile. There was strife with the Scots in

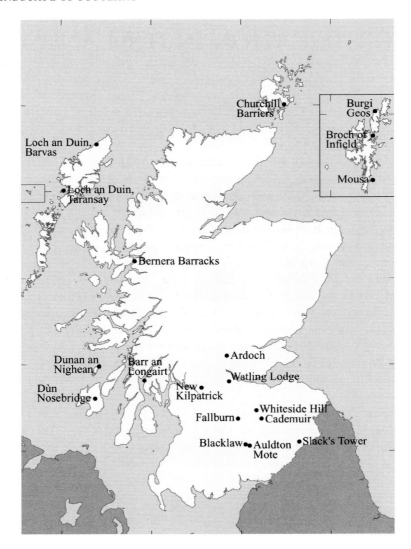

the west. Many excavated sites have been shown to be active at this time. One of the best known is included in a later chapter: Dunadd in Argyll, where there are documentary references to Pictish attacks on the stronghold and this was borne out by archaeological research.

In the eighth and ninth centuries the threats came once more from the outside as Norse raiders, or Vikings, made repeated incursions around the coastlands and came to dominate the lands of the north and west. Without excavation it is impossible to be certain that any particular site withstood Viking attack, but the abundance of defended sites in some areas would seem to speak for itself.

In 1066 the nature of government changed in England with the victory of William of Normandy over Harold. Though it must have seemed a remote victory, the repercussions were to reach Scotland and result in a new form of expression in the archaeological record. The Normans bought with them a new form of defence: the motte and bailey castle. Very soon castles such as this (Auldton) were being built in Scotland as the Scottish kings favoured Norman overlords who were granted lands in return for allegiance. The old ways were changing and the advantages of the old, topographical, fortifications were no longer apparent. Though life in Scotland did not settle down, and fortification remained an essential part of domestic architecture, the nature of that fortification changed over succeeding centuries. Small castles and tower houses served most defensive needs (Blacklaw and Slack's Tower).

In more recent years the nature of aggression has taken a different turn and new suites of military architecture have sprung up. The first hint of this came in the eighteenth century with the subduing of the Highlands by Government troops. The barracks at Bernera date from this period and they should be seen in conjunction with military roads such as that from Coupar Angus to Fort George in chapter 6. Though the military uses of many of these sites were short and limited, they were quickly adapted to other needs and remain an important element of the Scottish landscape today.

Scotland contains a wealth of more recent military remains and an oddity has been selected to remind us that the remains of war are not always obvious (the Churchill Barriers in Orkney from the Second World War). Like so many other military sites they are a good example of how peacetime value can endure long beyond the end of aggression. How many people, both Orcadians and visitors, take for granted the road to the Southern Isles that did not exist before the 1940s?

Broch of Infield: broch
Shetland, HU 453 747
HU47SE 1

At first glance there is no sign of any ancient monument in this photograph. The small lighthouse sits neatly astride a low rise on a short promontory with a well-preserved stone building to one side. Appearances, however, can be deceptive. The low rise masks the site of a broch, a squat tower-like structure which was common in Iron Age Scotland, especially in the north and west.

Brochs were a specialised form of building. They comprised dry-stone towers with a double thickness outer wall, windowless to the outside, and an open area in the centre where a timber roof would have protected a dwelling space. Many, though not necessarily all, rose to a height of as much as 14m. The best preserved, which gives a good idea of the almost intact structure of a broch, is in Shetland, at Mousa (*HU 457 236, HU42SE 1*). It is assumed that brochs were defensive in purpose. This would be in line with the generally perceived trend for increased aggression in the Iron Age, though there are several instances where the location of a broch was not of a primarily defensive nature. Brochs seem to have been a development in an age where circular buildings were the norm, and where elements of display and show were often as important as the need for defence.

The remains of the broch at Infield have now been reduced for the most part to a featureless mound of rubble, but closer inspection reveals stretches of outer facing and, at one time, small cells were also visible. Cells were a common feature in broch walls. In the 1930s deposits of midden, the domestic rubbish from the household who lived here, could be seen to be falling into the sea. Elsewhere, where brochs have been excavated, it

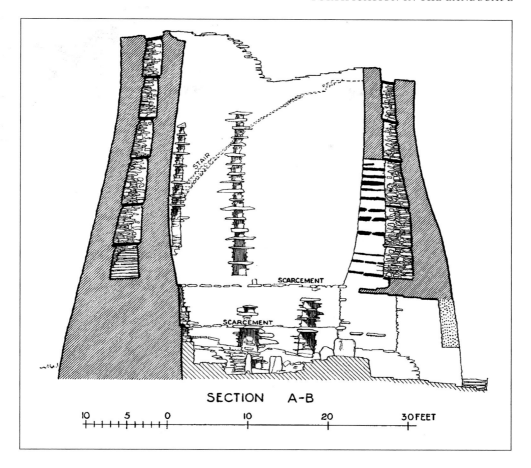

SECTION   A-B

has been shown that the interior space was often carefully subdivided, and in many cases, associated settlements of small circular stone dwellings were clustered around the outside of the main broch tower. These dwellings have been shown to contain many sophisticated features such as stone hearths and cupboards as well as toilets and drainage.

Brochs seem to have come into fashion in the first century BC, and most were out of use by the third century AD, though there are occasional indications of much later use. The most famous example of this is at Mousa where the Orkneyinga Saga records that Earl Erlend of Orkney took shelter in the broch with his lover in AD 1153. Given the impregnable nature of the broch structure, it is hardly surprising that the better-preserved buildings might still be useful.

The broch at Infield has never been excavated, so the details of its history are lacking. The coincidence of its location with the recent lighthouse, however, suggests that this was always an important spot from which to both control and aid local shipping. This is a feature of broch location that recurs elsewhere, notably in Orkney. Here, along the straits between Mainland and Rousay a series of brochs glare at each other across the narrows, the most famous being the Broch of Gurness and the Broch of Midhowe on either side of the water. At Infield the present appearance of the broch gives no sign of its former

glory. No doubt many of its stones have gone into the building of the stone house and its outbuildings: ancient structures have long been a good source of building stone. At the same time, the erection of the lighthouse on top of the broch remains cannot have done much for the preservation of its internal features. Together, however, the buildings in this photograph give a good idea of both continuity and surprise within the landscape.

Fallburn: fort
Lanarkshire, NS 961 367
NS93NE 6

The fort at Fallburn was built some 2000 years ago on a slight rise which offered little in the way of natural protection. The defences comprise two well-preserved ramparts, each with an outer ditch. The fort is almost exactly circular in plan, with two entrances, one to the north-east and one to the north-west. The remains of a stone wall run around the perimeter, inside the internal rampart, and this seems to be the result of strengthening or reconstruction work.

From the ground Fallburn is easy to see. From the air, however, a clearer image of the circular plan of this monument may be obtained, as also may some detail, such as of the internal wall. There is no trace of any internal structures, though a number of timber round houses would have stood here, providing both domestic dwellings for the community, as well as stores, animal byres and so on.

Fallburn today is located in ground that is very marginal for agriculture. The situation 2000 years ago was different, however. A combination of slightly better weather than today and less intensive farming methods meant that farming could continue higher up the hillsides and communities such as that at Fallburn would have reared stock as well as cultivated oats and barley in nearby fields. Wealth at the time was largely vested in cattle, and forts like this were an important part of the local scene, designed as much to safeguard the stock from predators, whether animals or people, as to protect their human population.

Barr an Longairt: fort
Argyll, NR 920 813
NR98SW 7

This small fort occupies a rocky crag on a ridge overlooking the eastern shores of Loch Fyne. A defensive wall may be discerned around the perimeter of the fort, though it is most pronounced on the eastern side where the fort would have been most vulnerable. To the west the sheer cliff of the crag provides a measure of natural protection. In places the massive blocks that made up the foundations of the wall can still be seen, but the photograph gives little indication of the original grandeur of its defences. This was a prominent local fort with a stout wall, nearly 3m wide. The main entrance to the enclosure lay on the east side where access was most easy, but there is also a small gap in the wall to the south-west.

There is no sign today of any buildings or internal structures within the fort. It is likely that these were built of timber to house both people and animals as well as to provide storage. Forts like this were used by small farming communities throughout the Iron Age, 2000 years

ago. They acted both as a defensive centre to protect against neighbourhood rivalries, and as a status symbol marking out the wealth and local position of their main occupants.

Other forts comprised defences on quite a different scale to the simplicity of the structure at Barr an Longairt. At Whiteside Hill in Peeblesshire (*NT 168 460, NT14NE 7*) a series of three prominent earthen ramparts and a stone wall represent at least three phases of occupation and remodelling (see **colour plate 19**). These have been ascribed to the pre-Roman Iron Age and the subsequent reoccupation of the fort after a period when it was abandoned during the Roman occupation. Inside the fort, indications of at least nine house-platforms have been recorded, and this must have been a community of some size.

Also in Peeblesshire lies the fort of Cademuir (*NT 224 370, NT23NW 12*) where the main defences comprise a stone wall with subsidiary enclosures. To the north-east of the fort, where it was clearly considered to have been at especial risk, over 100 sharply angled stones project out of the turf. These are the remains of a *chevaux de frise*, designed (no doubt successfully) to provide an obstacle especially to those advancing towards the fort on horseback. *Chevaux de frise* occur at other Scottish hill forts, but this is one of the best preserved, and it is also in an interesting location. It would have been quite invisible to an attacking force coming up from below. Not until they were right in amongst the stones would they have been aware of the trap that awaited them, and by then it was too late. The stones of Cademuir stand today as silent testimony to the guile of our ancestors, and it is hard not to imagine the scenes of conflict that drew them to make use of this carefully placed defence. Perhaps it is no coincidence that the local hills, including a higher summit at Cademuir itself, are scattered with the remains of other fortified settlements, and archaeologists have suggested that many of these may have been abandoned around the time of the Roman occupation. These fertile slopes also marked important routeways and there is bound to have been conflict between their occupants and the Roman incomers.

See **colour plate 19**

Dunan nan Nighean: dun
Colonsay, NR 415 976
NR49NW 5

Around 2700 years ago the techniques of working iron were introduced into Scotland. Everyday tools of the new metal were rare for many centuries, and it was reserved for special items such as jewellery and weapons. It is perhaps no coincidence that the Iron Age seems to have been a time of considerable instability, when specific communities were consolidating their power and local warfare was commonplace. In this atmosphere aggression and defence dominated the ways in which people lived, and many settlement sites were chosen for their defensive properties. Display was important too — it served to reinforce the identity of a community and to emphasize its importance compared to others. This could take place on a grand scale, in the erection of a particularly elaborate gateway to a prominent hill fort, for example, or on a smaller scale, with the purchase and wearing of costly jewellery. The new metal was well adapted for this sort of use and as such it oiled the wheels of Iron Age society.

Dunan nan Nighean on Colonsay is a typical example of the small, fortified farmsteads from this period that dot the Scottish landscape, particularly in the north and west, where the rocky outcrops and the local abundance of stone led to the construction of many sites like this. In principal, duns comprise a small stone-built round house in a defensive position, usually on a rocky boss. At Dunan nan Nighean a stone outwork was built across the more gentle eastern slopes of the hill. At the start of the twentieth century an internal stone hut was visible, but this seems to have been a relatively modern addition, and it was partly demolished in the 1940s when the site was excavated. The entrance to this site, as it appears today, is an impressive ruin, which stands out clearly in the landscape. It is

likely to be recent as well, however, presumably reflecting the long-standing interest and fascination in which sites like this have been held.

Duns were a good response to a long-term need. They continued to be built and used well into the Early Historic Period that succeeded the Roman occupation of the southern half of Scotland. Without detailed excavation and dating it is impossible to say whether any one structure, like Dunan nan Nighean, falls into the early or later period of their use. Duns also provide a uniquely personal link with the past because many were still in use well into times to which we can be transported by oral tradition. The names by which they are locally known are often very evocative. In this respect, Dunan nan Nighean translates as Dun of the Daughter which may not be very specific, but does add a personal touch to the site.

Loch an Duin, Taransay: crannog and dun
Western Isles, NB 021 012
NB00SW 6

The small stone island lying about 30m out into Loch an Duin, connected to the shore by a stone causeway, is the remains of a crannog or artificial island, constructed to support a building. Crannogs have a long antiquity in Scotland — some go back well into the Bronze Age — but they were most common in the Iron Age and Early Historic periods, and some were still in use well into the Middle Ages. Not surprisingly, given their long popularity, and the nature of the Scottish landscape with its numerous lochs and waterways, crannogs are a common feature of Scottish archaeology, though not all examples are as easy to see as this one.

At Loch an Duin the remains of stone walling can be made out rising from the water at the edge of the crannog. This is all that is left of the building that once occupied the island. In other areas timber buildings were more common, and even the basic structure of the crannog was often built of wood. There are many different types of crannog, but in the Western Isles the ready availability of stone, combined with the lack of timber, meant that stone was preferred. Similarly, crannog designs vary greatly. Many supported just one building, but some had more than one, and courtyards as well as animal pens have all been recorded. While some, as at Loch an Duin, were reached by causeway, others were cut off so that boats would have been necessary. In any case, the crannog dwellers were obviously quite at home on water, and boats must have played an important part in their lives. Another crannog site, also known as Loch an Duin, Barvas, Lewis (*NB 392 543, NB35SE 4*), photographed from the air, shows clearly the position of the causeway under water, and the remains of a stone building on the surface.

Archaeologists have long debated the reasons why water-based settlements became popular. Defence was no doubt an important factor, especially in a period such as the Iron Age where local rivalries could easily flare up, but in addition it is thought that by living in this way people could maximize their use of valuable farm lands. Clusters of crannogs are

often found in areas where fertile lands would have been quite restricted such as along the shores of the long inland lochs like Loch Tay. Furthermore, there is always the element of fashion — it is in human nature to covet, copy and improve on an idea once it has been shown to be useful. No doubt the reasons behind the building of many crannogs were complex mixtures of all three elements. In later periods crannogs were often recorded as high-status sites, still used by the local aristocracy well into the first millennium AD and used as much for feasting and entertainment as for refuge. They also provided very suitable prisons within which to confine your rivals!

Burgi Geos: promontory fort
Shetland, HP 478 033
HP40SE 1

Iron Age fortifications often made use of naturally inaccessible locations such as the steep promontories which abound along the coasts of the Northern Isles. At Burgi Geos in Shetland two lines of walling have been constructed across the neck of a sheer rocky promontory in order to provide defence to those who made this their home. The outer wall is built of large free-standing stones, while the inner structure is of a thicker build, known as a block-house. This survives to a greater height and at its southern end lies the position of the original entrance to the interior. There is no sign of any houses within the interior, but the remains of a stone wall enclose the top of the cliffs, apparently to give added reassurance to the inhabitants (and no doubt to stop small children and others from falling into the sea).

Promontory forts are common around the coasts of Scotland and they were a frequent feature of the landscape at least from the Iron Age on into Pictish times. It is hard to imagine anyone living in these precipitous locations, but they must have provided shelter to many families. In the days before motorized transport these locations were not particularly remote. Their close proximity to the sea meant that they were mainstream

Ancient Brough (fortification) on the Burgie Geos West Neaps North Yell

spots for a people to whom the boat was a rapid and flexible form of transport. In contrast to the peaceful sounds of the waves on the rocks that are experienced by the modern visitor, the visitor in the past would have heard the sounds of settlement: dogs; children; adult voices; as well as cattle in the nearby fields. No doubt the soothing smells of sea and grass would have been replaced by something more earthy too, as the visitor approached the areas of domestic refuse.

Ardoch: Roman fort
Perthshire, NN 839 099
NN80NW 10

Some archaeological sites, though up-standing, are of such an impressive size that it is hard to make sense of them on the ground. In these cases an aerial photograph can provide a clear view of the site in its entirety and also put its context within its present-day landscape. Ardoch Roman fort is one of these sites.

Ardoch is not only impressive by Scottish standards, it has been described as 'one of the most impressive forts in the Roman Empire' (Walker & Ritchie, 1996, 151). Parts of the complex system of ramparts here look almost as if they were dug recently, though they have undergone the blurring effects of nearly two millennia. Like many Roman fortifications, the fort at Ardoch has a complicated history and was built and altered over a number of years. Its early occupation has been dated to the Flavian period around the

end of the first century AD, and the later alterations seem to have taken place in the Antonine period around AD 150. Ardoch has been identified as a fort known as Alauna in Ptolemy's Geography, and one of the military units garrisoned here in the early phase has been identified as the *cohors I Hispanorum*. The fort was excavated in the 1890s and this, together with recent geophysical survey work, has revealed that traces of several buildings remain inside.

Ardoch lies at the southern end of a strategic system of timber watch towers that was placed alongside a Roman road that ran the length of the Gask Ridge, a prominent natural feature in the Perthshire landscape. These watchtowers were supplemented by at least one fortlet, at Kaims Castle, as well as two larger forts at Strageath and Bertha. The Gask Ridge was one of the earliest land frontiers of the Roman Empire. Though it did not have a continuous physical line of demarcation, as did the later frontiers of the Antonine Wall and Hadrian's Wall, it was designed as a sophisticated boundary. Forts like Ardoch housed a substantial garrison and there was also provision for other personnel. In addition to assisting control over the native peoples both inside and outside Roman territory, the Roman frontier systems provided a means of swift communication for the troops through both signal systems and well-built roads. They also served an important economic purpose, however, allowing the Roman bureaucracy to oversee matters like taxes, tribute and even local markets. In this way Ardoch worked not only to defend the boundaries of empire but also to bolster local control within the frontier zone of central Scotland.

Roman work on the forts of the Gask Ridge seems to have started in the early 80s during a campaign of consolidation in southern Scotland. In time, however, as Roman bureaucratic and military needs in this far northern boundary of empire changed, the towers of the Gask Ridge were abandoned and attention turned to the construction of more ambitious frontier walls further south.

The strategic importance of the siting of the fort at Ardoch is emphasized by the fact that several other camps, each dating to difference episodes of the Roman occupation of Scotland, were built in this area, though each was only briefly used. Two of these camps, to the west of the fort, and dating to the campaigns of Septimus Severus in the early years of the third century AD, may be made out above ground in places, but mostly they are visible only through the use of aerial photography. Many Roman camps were in use only for a very short space of time — weeks or even days — and it is amazing to think that such short activity has left a permanent mark on the landscape of Scotland. All were carefully built by Roman standards. The soldiers dug good defences and the internal arrangements were laid out according to set plans.

New Kilpatrick: the Antonine Wall
Dumbartonshire, NS 556 723
NS57SE 42

The Antonine Wall was constructed on the orders of the Roman Emperor Antoninus Pius in the first half of the second century AD. It comprised a turf rampart running across the Forth-Clyde isthmus with regularly sited forts to house a garrison and frequent small watchtowers. A road ran behind it. The Antonine Wall superceded Hadrian's Wall, which lay further to the south, but it was only in use for a few years. The evidence suggests that the Antonine Wall was finally abandoned by AD 170.

The Wall was built in sections by three legions of the Roman Army. It was a highly organized affair, with each legion working on a separate stretch. For most of its length the Wall was built of turf, which was set onto a stone foundation, and a deep ditch lay to the front (northern) side. There may have been a timber palisade along the top. On the south side of the Wall a road was built, within Roman territory.

The Antonine Wall made an impressive physical barrier, clearly dividing the Roman Empire from the barbaric lands to the north. The sophisticated signalling system and ease of communications along the road eased the task of the troops who were stationed here to defend the frontier from the tribes outside. The Wall also served other purposes, however. The Roman population included civilian officials as well as families who travelled with the soldiers. By providing some security for these people, the Antonine Wall worked to reinforce Roman control over those who lived within the frontier lands. The local

population was not always happy to accept Roman subjugation, so that economic control, through methods such as taxation and the supervision of the movement and sale of goods, was a subtle way in which to retain Roman authority.

At New Kilpatrick the Wall runs through the modern cemetery and two sections of the stone base have been preserved and laid out. It is perhaps a surprising location for an ancient monument, but it is a good reminder of how the use of the land can change. The careful construction of the base is evident in the evenly set cobbles with their edging stones, and in the culverts which provide drainage.

Despite its location in the heartland of the Scottish Central Belt several stretches of the Wall are still visible. A good idea of the state of preservation of the turf rampart and ditch can be seen at Watling Lodge, Falkirk (*NS 862 797, NS87NE 7*), where the Wall passes the site of a small fortlet. Though it has been reduced and in-filled by erosion and deposition, and by the growth of trees, the Wall is still a formidable feature in the landscape here.

103

There have been many excavations along the length of the Wall. Those at the fort of Rough Castle, Stirlingshire in the 1950s provided clear photographic evidence for the placing of the turves over the stone foundations. Experimental archaeology here in the 1890s, by the Glasgow Archaeology Society demonstrated that the original height of the turves was likely to have been over 3m.

Dùn Nosebridge: fortification
Islay, NR 371 601
NR36SE 10

The construction of fortifications within ramparts was not something that stopped with the coming of the Romans. Many earlier types of site — forts, duns and crannogs — continued in use both during and after the Roman incursions into southern Scotland. In many cases it is impossible to tell the date of a site from surface analysis alone, so that analogy with information from excavated sites is needed. Elsewhere there are differences, sometimes subtle, sometimes glaringly obvious, that point to some sort of architectural development over time.

Dùn Nosebridge in Islay is a site that seems to have some developmental changes and these have been interpreted by archaeologists as suggesting a later, post-Roman date. Though it bears a superficial similarity to many Iron Age forts, it is a very unusual site. This is an impressive fortification. On initial inspection it comprises a series of well-preserved earth and rubble ramparts that defends a rectangular central citadel. The hillside has been formed into flat terraces behind each of the ramparts so that it has a pyramid-like profile that stands prominently apart from its surroundings. There is no outward sign of the internal arrangements of the fort, but various timber structures, including dwellings, byres and stores would be expected. Similarly, the identity of the builders has long since been lost, but it is at sites like this that the status of the fort as an important central place as well as a place of refuge can best be appreciated. It is likely that the builders of Dùn Nosebridge represented a family of some standing.

Despite the general similarity of the defences to other Iron Age forts, Dùn Nosebridge may well be a more recent defensive structure, making use of the age-old technique of throwing up a series of earthen ramparts in order to defend its central citadel. In this respect it perhaps bears more relation to a local adaptation of the practice of building earthwork motte and bailey castles that was imported into Scotland in the eleventh and twelfth centuries. Whatever the date of its construction, Dùn Nosebridge is an impressive monument, and the enigmas surrounding its date and precise nature highlight the attractions of archaeology — there is always something more to find out. Surprisingly, this is true even on obvious sites such as Dùn Nosebridge.

Auldton Mote: motte and bailey
Dumfriess-shire, NT 093 058
NT00NE 14

Hidden amongst trees and scrub on the outskirts of Moffat stands the motte and bailey castle of Auldton. The motte, or central mound, still stands to a height of 8m, though it has been somewhat damaged by antiquarian trenching in times past. This mound would have formed the heart of the castle, supporting a timber tower, or lookout, that usually also provided accommodation for the family of the local lord. Around the tower there is likely to have been a timber palisade at the edge of the motte, which then slopes steeply down to a ditch that survives to a depth of nearly 2m. To the south-west there is an enclosed area known as the bailey. This housed a range of domestic buildings, also built of wood. These buildings would have provided a place for the retainers and their families, as well as stabling, stores, and workshops. Around the bailey there is an earthwork bank, that would originally have been surmounted by another palisade. There is an external ditch which would have been crossed by a timber bridge at the entrance, which was probably to the north-west.

Motte and baileys are early castles. This style of fortification was brought to Britain from France and most castles of this type were raised in the years following the Norman conquest of England in 1066. The earthworks and timber structures could be raised very quickly; it is recorded that some took as little as eight days to build. In the unsettled years that followed the Norman Conquest this was a very useful method by which troops could be deployed across the country to enforce Norman rule.

Not surprisingly motte and bailey castles were also deployed in Scotland. Here they served to reinforce the influence of the Crown as sympathetic lords and nobles were given lands, together with the right to build and garrison a castle. Their influence worked to extend central rule across the country.

Auldton motte lies at the centre of the photo. The curving bank outside the bailey may be seen with a few scrubby trees, and to the right the steep mound of the motte rises up inside slightly denser woodland. Many motte and bailey castles were later adapted with stone defences which replaced the timber works. Auldton, however, seems to have remained as a timber castle so that only its earthworks remain. Today it is respected by the local agriculture, but the flat ground inside the bailey has traces of rig and furrow cultivation showing that there was a time when this was not so. In the background stands a row of fine suburban houses — Auldton is a good example of how good-quality archaeological remains may still be found even at the heart of a relatively recent urban landscape.

Blacklaw: tower
Dumfriess-shire, NT 052 067
NT00NE 3

Many archaeological sites look like nothing more than a heap of stones when you first catch site of them. Closer inspection, however, can reveal a wealth of detail that provides clues as to their original purpose, form and date. Blacklaw Tower is a good example of this. Most of the site is concealed by a turf covered mound, but some architectural details including an arch and dressed stonework suggest that this was once a building of some status.

The mound conceals the remains of a sixteenth-century tower house that survives to first-floor level. It is now in a very ruinous state: the ground-floor vault is recorded as quite unstable and the first floor is only represented by the lower courses of the walls, with the traces of a window on the south-east side. An internal stair gave access from the ground-floor entrance to the upper levels. Around the tower lie the remains of an enclosure and several other buildings, most of which, like a kitchen range to the south-east, are probably contemporary with the tower. Possible traces of an earlier defensive structure have also been recognized.

Although Blacklaw was not an elaborately defended structure, it is a typical tower house of its time. The sixteenth century was a period of general unrest, particularly in the borderlands between Scotland and England, when individual families had to guard against cattle thieving and other rivalry. The fact that anyone was as likely to initiate raids as to receive them only added to matters. The lands of Blacklaw are first recorded in the early fourteenth century, when King Robert I granted them to Sir David de Lyndsay of Crawford. In the following years they changed hands several times, a sign of the general unrest. In 1510 they passed to the Herries family of Terregles, and they were then re-granted to the Maxwells before being made over to the Johnstons who later sold them to Lieutenant-Colonel William Johnston, a younger son of the First Earl of Hartfell.

The tower itself was built in the sixteenth century and the position was carefully chosen. It lies on level ground in a bend of the burn which drops at this point into a steep gully. Today the surrounding lands are covered by forestry but this masks the nature of the landscape in which Blacklaw was built. Traces of past cultivation dotted within the forest plantings provide an indication of a very different landscape in which the local population could be largely self-sufficient.

Slack's Tower: pele-house and archaeological landscape
Roxburghshire, NT 644 098
NT60NW 3

The ruined building in the picture may not look particularly imposing, and today it stands in an empty landscape, but things were not always so here. The present ruins represent the extensive remains of a well-to-do Border farm from the sixteenth century, and there are other indications of earlier buildings that provide evidence for the antiquity of settlement here.

The upstanding remains comprise the structure of a pele-house, or defensive farm. It now stands to two storeys high, and there are indications of an attic floor. Typically for such buildings the ground floor is windowless to aid defence, but two windows survive at first-floor level. There are extensive structural remains around the pele, some of which relate to out-buildings and other dwellings contemporary with the tower, while others relate

111

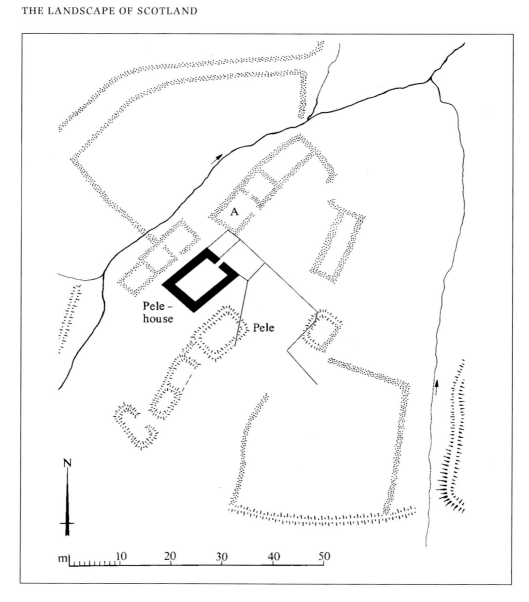

to earlier remains. There are also various enclosures, and further afield the undulating remains of rig and furrow cultivation stretch over some 5.5ha. These were fertile lands. At the edge of the lands of Slack's Tower there is a well-preserved boundary bank, or head dyke, with an external ditch. This would have served as much to keep animals off the cultivated lands as to provide a marker for the human population. Friendly neighbours were not something you could always rely upon.

The settlement at Slack's Tower was mapped by Pont in the seventeenth century and subsequently marked on the map by Blaeu, using Pont's data, in 1654. In 1691 the local Hearth Tax Return lists three hearths here, but by the eighteenth century the community had disappeared from the maps altogether. At this time the combination of a series of

112

bad winters together with the introduction of new farming methods meant that many settlements like this were abandoned. The landscape, however, was not completely emptied at first. A number of drystone enclosures built over the earlier remains attest to the presence in the vicinity of sheep and their shepherds.

With time even sheep farming became a less intensive occupation so that the land assumed its current air of desertion. Forestry encroaches to the east, an indication for future generations of our present policies and preoccupations. Only the humps and bumps of the archaeological remains, together with the unprepossessing structure of the pele-house, provide a reminder of the noise, colour and life that once rang out through the valley.

Bernera, Glenelg: military barracks
Inverness-shire, NG 815 197
NG81NW 5

This unprepossessing building comprises the remains of the military barracks at Bernera, built in 1722 to provide a base for the Government troops stationed in the Highlands after the Jacobite Rising of 1715. The site was selected for its strategic importance at one of the main crossing points on the important routeway between Skye and the mainland of Scotland. The barracks were commissioned in 1719, but before work could begin there was another, abortive, uprising and construction did not start until 1720.

The building cost £2,444 17s and it was designed to house 240 men in five bedded dormitories set into two large gabled blocks. These were joined into a quadrangle by fortified ramparts and there was a well, together with a bake- and brew-house, latrines, and a guard house. In practice, however, there were never more than 150 men here and the barracks are recorded as having more influence on the local civilian population than on those who were fomenting possible unrest. They held too few men to play an active role in the uprising of 1745 and in later years the Barrack-Masters were frequently called upon to lend a hand at the local school.

The active life of Bernera Barracks was a short one. By the 1770s the garrison was substantially reduced, and in 1786 when Bernera was visited by John Knox he recorded that the only residents were a couple — an old corporal and his wife. In 1797 the land on which they were built was returned to MacLeod of MacLeod, from whom it had been bought, and they went out of service. The building was still in reasonable condition, however, and it played an important role in the nineteenth century in housing local families, especially those who had been evicted from their land. It is recorded that a room at Bernera could be rented for 20/- a year (Miket 1998).

Bernera Barracks was one of four barrack sites, built and garrisoned in the Highlands by the Government army in the early eighteenth century. All were placed at strategic positions on major routeways where there was already an existing garrison. The others were at Inversnaid, Kiliwhimen and Ruthven. The planning of these barracks was an important strategy in the control of the Highlands after the 1715 uprising when the Hanoverian Government in London realized just how fragile its hold was over the north of Scotland. They sought both to house troops across the country and to inform themselves better about the nature of the land and its occupants. As a part of this the Military Survey of Scotland took place later in the eighteenth century to produce land maps under the leadership of William Roy, and coastal charts were prepared by Murdoch Mackenzie, Hydrographer to the Admiralty. Roy's maps have become an important source of information on the state of the land in the mid-eighteenth century.

See **colour plate 20**

Churchill Barriers: naval blockships and military causeway
Orkney, HY 484 010
HY40SE 25

The large concrete blocks in the foreground form part of one of the four causeways that were built between the southern islands of Orkney in the 1940s to prevent access to the sheltered harbour of Scapa Flow during the Second World War. Scapa Flow was of great strategic importance as a safe anchorage for the British fleet.

In the First World War Scapa Flow had also been important and attempts to protect it were made by sinking a series of blockships in the approaches to the Flow. Most of these were subsequently salvaged or destroyed, but the remains of two remain above water, one of which, an unnamed steamship built in 1887, can be seen in the photograph. The blockships were only a partial success and early in the Second World War a German U-Boat, the U47, got into the Flow and torpedoed HMS Royal Oak which sank with the loss of 834 lives.

Work on the barriers was started by Churchill in 1940, hence their name. Although the distances to be covered were not great, it was a tricky task, due to the depth of water between the islands and the rapid tidal currents. The first stage was to sink rubble and after this huge concrete blocks were laid; eventually this was capped with a tarmac road surface. The blocks had to be specially cast for the purpose, and there were over 66,000 of them, each weighing 5 or 10 tons. Much, but not all, of the work was done by prisoners of war, mainly Italians, who were housed in barracks on the neighbouring islands. Most of the upstanding remains of their camps are long gone, though the grass covered footings may still be made out — an interesting archaeological site in themselves.

Today the Barriers are still in place, though they need constant maintenance. They are spanned by the modern road and now have an important role as the main artery of communication between the Mainland of Orkney and the Southern Isles. Though not, perhaps, foreseen by their builders, they have had far-reaching effects on the cultural and economic life of Orkney by providing easy, year-round access throughout the southern part of the chain of islands.

Scapa Flow is still an important place, not only as a sheltered strategic harbour, but also for its remains. At the end of the First World War Scapa Flow was used as a safe anchorage for the German High Seas Fleet which had been interned there. However, on 21 June 1919 the German Admiral gave orders for each ship to be scuttled. A group of Orkney school children happened to be out in a dinghy at the time and the sight of the ships slowly sinking is still remembered today. The ships of the German Fleet joined the many wrecks that had built up in Scapa Flow over the years. Since then there has been a certain amount of diving for study and for salvage work.

Scapa Flow today is a war grave, so that modern diving and recreation here is carefully controlled. It serves as an important reminder that archaeological remains do not stop at the tide mark. Material that has survived underwater is just as important as land-based material, sometimes more so because of the better preservation conditions that can prevail.

See **colour plate 21**

5 INDUSTRY IN THE LANDSCAPE

Scotland is rich in natural resources and throughout her history and prehistory she has provided handsomely for the needs of her inhabitants. In any consideration of the impact of industry on the landscape of Scotland it is important to remember that the definition of 'industry' has been relative over time. In the past Scotland has played an important role as an industrial nation. This is due largely to the combination of abundant resources with suitable topography for the transport of finished goods and materials, and with sources of power. Many industrial techniques were developed here, but today all has changed. The earlier workings would hardly be considered industrial by modern standards, while even the more easily recognized industrial sites of the past have often decayed to such an extent that it is hard to accept the industrial foundations of today's rural landscape. The flint quarry-pits of our prehistoric ancestors at Den of Boddam appear to us to be small-scale and local in comparison to the slate quarries at Ballachulish, though their impact on the prehistoric Scots would have been just as far-reaching in their own way.

Over time, the needs of the inhabitants of Scotland have changed, and with the growing population so has the scale of those needs. At the same time, a slow but constant increase in knowledge of available resources was combined with developing technology to allow the extraction and processing of new materials. It is no coincidence that many of the major developments of the industrial revolution took place here. In the eighteenth century, the coincidence of abundant timber to provide power, local iron ore supplies, and long sea-lochs for easy transport provided just the right conditions for the burgeoning iron industry. This was an important attraction for the teams of English iron-masters who moved into Scotland to develop their craft.

The iron industry has been crucial throughout much of Scottish history and it is a good example of development and change in the archaeological remains. The earliest sites, such as the bloomery at Cluan, would scarcely be recognized by a passer-by today. Even later sites like that at Furnace, though important when they were in use, are hardly given much attention these days and few visitors to the area throw a second glance over the derelict sheds at the heart of the village. More recently, in the eighteenth and nineteenth centuries, the scale of working changed yet again to cover whole tracts of landscape (Wilsontown). In these areas, though they are easier for the casual observer to see, there has been little attempt to preserve and interpret the remains because of the generally low value that is placed on recent industrial material by society today.

In fact, well-preserved large-scale industrial landscapes are rare. They have been hit by the approaches of other land uses such as blanket forestry (itself an industrial landscape, albeit a more recent one), housing or farmland. Industrial landscapes are an important archaeological resource in their own right. With the changes in the industrial and economic

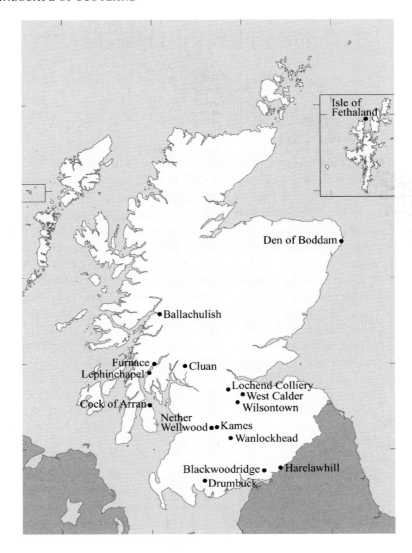

base of Scotland that took place in the twentieth century, landscapes such as that at Kames, Muirkirk are no longer created. Their management and recording is vital if we are not to lose this valuable facet of our past.

It is important to recognize the value of industrial remains and make sure that the monuments do not go unrecorded. How will future generations regard the empty site of a super-quarry, or the extensive foundations of a science park? As the economic basis of the country has changed so has the nature of industry. The remains at Wanlockhead provide a good example of this. Here a previous extractive industry has become part of the modern tourist industry which in itself may soon become a feature of the archaeological record.

Industry does not only relate to the extraction and production of goods. It also relates to other processes. The scale of the widespread forestry industry in the late twentieth-century Scotland has been noted. On a smaller scale, the salt works at Cock of Arran gives a good example of an early food-related industrial site. Though salt production today occurs well away from the consideration of most of us, this has not always been so. Salt production in the eighteenth century took place at a more local level and most people would have been aware of the origins of salt and of its value as a commodity. The transformation of salt into a commonplace material that comes from a middleman (today's supermarket) mirrors that of so many other necessities of life. How many children today relate their school milk to a field of cows?

Industry provides a good example of a further element of the archaeological landscape. This is in the use of place-names. Place-names relate to many different things and they can round out our understanding of the landscape (Nicholaisen 1976). Names can provide both specific and ethnic information. Many place-names are derived from topography, as in the gaelic use of *cnoc* for a knoll or hillock: Knock Bay in Skye. Some names relate simply to individuals or groups, such as the Pictish element *pit* in places like Pitcarmick. Others relate to management issues, like *achadh*, a gaelic name meaning field: Achnahaird. Names have related to individual buildings such as the *kirk* or *kil* (church) names: Kilmory Oib. Names may concern events such as the meeting of a Norse parliament or *ting*: Dingwall in Ross-shire. Finally, there are names that provide information on past uses, such as Furnace in Argyll. Even today there is scope for new names: Livingston for example celebrates nineteenth-century achievement. Thus we add our own layer to the parchment of the landscape. Place-names provide a good indication that all is not as it has been across the face of Scotland.

In some cases the steatite quarries cover a considerable area. That at Fethaland is one of the biggest in Shetland. It is also interesting to note that blanks were occasionally discarded after being roughed out; we can only speculate as to why, whether they did not conform to standards, or whether their makers got called away. Broken bowls are also found; it is clear that the steatite workers of the past were only human — they had bad days and made mistakes, just as we do today. Finding the mistakes is one of the joys of archaeology for it links you to the past at a very personal level!

Steatite was also used in lesser quantities in earlier periods, though no earlier workings have as yet been recognized. It was sometimes transported away from the islands of Shetland. In Orkney, a Bronze Age cemetery at Lingafold contained a large steatite vessel which had been used to contain a cremation. The raw material for this was imported by boat from Shetland. Steatite vessels also occur into the early medieval period, though by then the use of the quarries was gradually reducing.

It is very difficult to date quarry sites without the excavation of associated working floors where datable artefacts may have been lost, or where hearths can provide carbon for radiocarbon assay. The shape of the bowls that were removed can provide a clue and it is likely that quarries such as that at Fethaland date back to Viking times some 1100 years ago.

Lephinchapel: charcoal-burning platforms
Argyll, NR 964 896
NR98NE 5

Traces of some 60 flat platforms have been recorded on this hillside overlooking Loch Fyne. Each platform has been carefully scooped into the hillside and the upcast used to form an apron, thus producing a level area. Though the area today bears only sparse woodland, these platforms indicate that there was once a greater cover of trees here for they provided the stances upon which sat the pyres from charcoal burning.

Platforms such as these would have been a common sight in the Scottish woodlands from prehistory well into the eighteenth century. Charcoal was a versatile fuel that played an important role in the development of industry in Scotland. It was particularly useful for the smelting of metals, and as the demand for iron grew, so the number of charcoal platforms multiplied across the wooded hillsides.

123

The production of charcoal from wood took place at specific times of the year. It was a skilled process that ran hand in hand with the careful management of the woodlands. Though timber was required, it was necessary to ensure that the hillsides were not completely cleared of trees as the wood was harvested for burning. The trees were therefore coppiced to provide branches of the right size while allowing for regeneration. The timber was built into a domed pyre which would ensure the precise conditions to reduce the wood to charcoal without burning it completely. Individual groups of charcoal burners each worked in set territories. They would commonly have several pyres alight at any one time and each required careful tending.

The platforms provided a stable base for each pyre, but excavation of selected platforms in this group has revealed that they also served other functions. The burners needed shelter while they worked, and some of the platforms supported round timber dwelling-huts in the temporary camps that were set up. It is likely that different groups of platforms were revisited on a rotational basis, in order to allow for regeneration of the woodland. The purpose of individual platforms thus changed as they were reused for burning in later years.

Charcoal was also useful in other industries. It was an important source of acetone and acetic acid, but in all processes its useful lifespan was limited. In the iron industry it was taken over in importance by coke. With time, the demand for charcoal fell and so the platforms went out of use. Once this happened, it was no longer so important to maintain the woodland which suffered, ironically, from both neglect and from felling. Some woodlands became overcrowded as old dead wood was no longer removed; others disappeared as regeneration was no longer important. Throughout the later eighteenth and nineteenth centuries the shift in emphasis to hillside grazing for both sheep and red deer removed much of the young growth so that the trees could no longer regenerate. Over time the woodlands reduced to such an extent that it is often hard to imagine that there were ever enough trees to be worked in an area such as this. Today, the charcoal-burning platforms stand in mute testimony to an altered landscape.

Cock of Arran: salt works
Isle of Arran, NR 971 511
NR95SE 1

Salt has always been an important commodity, and production in the past was generally carried out by the sea, at a relatively small, local scale. The buildings at Cock of Arran stand away from modern settlement, but they represent the remains of a small salt works run between 1710-35 by the Dukes of Hamilton who owned the land. It is reported that the Hamiltons brought in colliers and salt workers from Bo'ness on the Firth of Forth in the East of Scotland where there were extensive Hamilton-owned coal mines and other salt works.

The impetus for the salt production here was the discovery of low grade coal which could be mined on the spot and used to fuel the pan-house. At least two derelict mine shafts have been recognized among the remains. The pan-house stood by the shore so that sea water could easily be taken in to boil off the water and leave the salt as a residue. There would have been an iron pan, some 5.5m x 2.5m set over a furnace. The furnace itself was stoked and controlled from the fore-house which stood immediately behind the pan-house and probably incorporated a bothy for the salters on its upper floor. The terraced remains of workers' cottages from the coal mining may also be seen just further

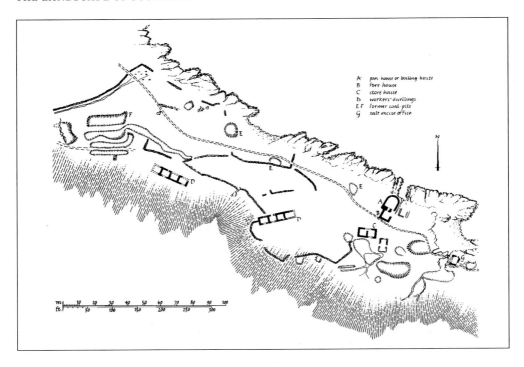

along the shore here. Other remains include a two-roomed storehouse, built in 1712, and a small building which is set apart and has been identified as possibly the office for the salt Excisemen.

The local coal supplies were quickly used up, bringing an abrupt halt to salt production in 1735. In the 1770s the coal mines were once again reopened for a while, but salt production was not restarted, though the abandoned buildings seem to have survived largely unaltered apart from the decay of the centuries.

Cluan: bloomery
Stirlingshire, NS 366 977
NS39NE 5

Low mounds like this abound in previously wooded areas of the Highlands, though they are gradually disappearing under the pressures of recent land management schemes such as modern forestry. At first sight they do not appear to be of any great interest, but closer inspection usually reveals small quantities of iron slag and sometimes charcoal in their vicinity and this is the clue to their origin. These are the remains of bloomeries, where iron was smelted on a small scale.

Bloomeries like this were still in use in the seventeenth century, though some may be much earlier. This was a small-scale industry, producing iron for local consumption. The raw material generally comprised bog-ore, which could be dug up from many spots throughout the Highlands. The iron smelting was closely tied in to the management of woodlands and the production of charcoal. The furnace was very simple: a shallow hollow scooped into the ground, and the burning of local charcoal would suffice to produce enough heat for the ore to be reduced into a lump of iron, known as a 'bloom'.

The melting temperature of iron is 1540C, and it was hard for a furnace such as this to be properly controlled to ensure a constant heat. The iron bloom, therefore, though malleable, was often full of impurities and it required repeated reheating and hammering in order to create a purer metal. By smelting the iron with charcoal the iron masters were, intentionally or unintentionally, producing a much improved product. The addition of small amounts of carbon, less than 0.5%, greatly increases the strength of the metal, thereby rendering it more versatile for tools and weapons. If it was also quenched (cooled rapidly in cold water) the iron could be made harder still, though care had to be taken or it would become too brittle. In order to avoid this, the metal was then gently reheated to a lower temperature. This is one of the reasons why a good supply of water has always been particularly important for a blast furnace.

With time the iron industry became more sophisticated. The technology of producing iron in a charcoal-fired blast furnace was developed in England but the iron masters quickly realized that Scotland, with plentiful charcoal and water as well as local supplies of bog iron and good water-borne transport, was well suited to the development of the industry. The first blast furnaces in Scotland were built in the early years of the eighteenth century and bloomery sites, such as the one in the photograph, became a thing of the past. Their remains survive, however, as a telling reminder that, in an age where life was less centralized, even small communities were quite capable of undertaking basic industrialized processes. The sharp divisions that we experience today between rural and industrial were once quite blurred.

1   *Cùl a' Bhaile: hut circle*

2   *Hill of Alyth: ring-ditch house*

3   Gibbs Hill: palisaded settlement

4   Ven Law: settlement

5   *Pitcarmick Loch: sub-rectangular building*

6   *Dun Borrafiach: shieling mound*

7   *Greod, Sanday:*
deserted settlement

8   *Unish House:*
tacksman's house

9 *Grumby:*
   farmstead and
   stackyard

10 *Holyrood Park:*
    cultivation
    terraces

11 *Tomnagaoithe: kiln barn*

12 *Carn Bhithir: illicit whisky still*

13 Callanish: peat cuttings and antiquarian diggings

14 Buzzart Dikes: deer park

15 & 16 Orval: deer trap

17   (right) Conagearaidh: kelp kiln

18   (far right) Kinloch, Rum: castle policies

19   (below right) Whiteside Hill: fort

20   *Bernera, Glenelg: military barracks*

21   *Churchill Barriers: naval blockships and military causeway*

22   *Den of Boddam: flint mines and workings*

23   *Harelawhill: limestone quarries and lime works*

24   *Dunadd: entrance to the fort*

25   *Kilchattan, Luing: ship graffiti*

26   *Garvamore, Inverness-shire: Wade bridge for the military road*

27   *Wormy hillock: henge*

28 Cononbridge: henge

29 Ballymeanoch: standing stones

30   Sgorr nam Ban-
      Naomha: cashel

31   Creich: cross

32 *Kilchoan:*
chambered tomb

33 *Conagearaidh:*
old burial
ground and
settlement

Furnace, Craleckan Ironworks: blast furnace
Argyll, NN 025 000
NN00SW 11

The buildings in the photograph are remarkably well preserved, though they occupy the heart of a small village on the shores of Loch Fyne. Their rural location offers little indication, on the surface, of their original purpose. Some 250 years ago, however, the tranquility of this spot would have been replaced by something very different. Together with other locations scattered through the Highlands this would have been one of the most industrialized parts of Scotland. The industrialization was not heavy by our standards, but at the time when it operated it would have been remarkable. The now peaceful shores of Loch Fyne once witnessed the heat, noise and colour of metallurgy, for this is the location of one of Scotland's earliest blast furnaces, home to the burgeoning iron industry.

The furnace and its associated buildings were constructed in 1755 by the Argyll Furnace Co, an offshoot of an English company from Lancashire. There were already other furnaces in operation in Argyll; at Glen Kinglass operations ran from 1722-38 and at Bonawe work started in 1753. The Craleckan Ironworks only operated for some 60 years, it went out of use around 1813, but the buildings remain remarkably intact. The lining of the hearth has lain untouched since the furnace was last fired up.

The builders of Craleckan chose their spot carefully. Proximity to Loch Fyne ensured water transport, vital both to import iron ore from England and to export the finished product. There was abundant woodland nearby to be carefully managed by coppicing in order to provide a plentiful supply of locally produced charcoal for fuel, and there was a water supply to turn a wheel which drove a pair of great bellows to provide the draft

129

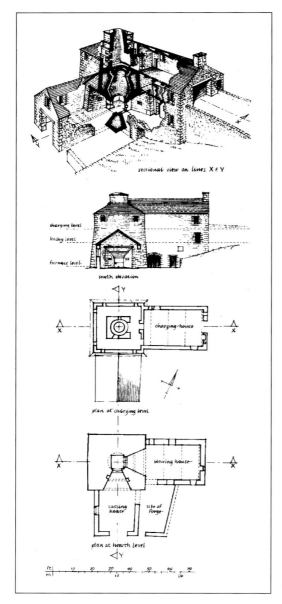

sectional view on lines X & Y

charging level
bothy level
furnace level

south elevation

charging-house

plan at charging level

blowing house

casting house   site of forge

plan at hearth level

for the fire. The surrounding structures include a two-storey building to house the charcoal, ore and limestone prior to charging on its upper floor, while the lower floor housed the bellows. To the south there was a single-storey casting house where the molten iron would be run off into troughs in a bed of sand to form bars of pig iron. Besides this there was a forge where some of the pig iron could be refined and worked into wrought iron before export. In addition, a community of dwellings and ancillary buildings sprang up, to provide for the needs of the workers.

Today, Furnace survives as a small village, though there is little sign of its former status as a part of Scotland's industrial heartland. Elsewhere, at Bonawe, the community also included housing, a church and a school, but today the village has gone. At Glen Kinglass there is even less sign of the community that once throve on the shores of Loch Etive. In this way, iron smelting provides a wonderful example of how the countryside has changed. In the eighteenth century the areas round the iron works must have been some of the most industrialized in Scotland. They would have seemed quite alien to the rural passer-by, and even the visitor from the cities would have been surprised at the activity, noise and heat. Yet today these locations are well away from the areas that we would consider industrialized. Indeed, some lie in lands that would be regarded as prime wilderness country, such as the northern shores of Loch Maree in Wester Ross. It is a sobering lesson to learn that the power of human contact can be swept away so easily, but it should also bring hope with the realisation that nature can still take back even quite industrialized land, though it is never, of course, quite the same again.

Wilsontown: ironworks, coal pits, workers housing, lime kilns
Lanarkshire, NS 950 549
NS95SE 11

The Wilsontown Ironworks was established in 1779 by two brothers, John and William Wilson from Carnwath. They had done very well from their business in trade between London and Sweden, and sought to invest some of their capital nearer to home. The ideal opportunity was presented by the local burn, the Mouse Water, where seams of coal, limestone and ironstone were available. Large quantities of raw materials were not necessary and so the Wilson brothers set to work to construct a furnace making use of the most up-to-date technology. Their ironworks was a successful venture and over the next 30 years it flourished so that by 1794 there was a substantial local community housing 400 people. By 1812 the community amounted to over 2000, of whom 521 men were employees of the company, but growth at this scale could not continue forever. The business suffered from problems, and in the early nineteenth century the ironworks was closed and put up for sale.

We can only speculate on the hardships of life here while a new purchaser was sought, but in 1821 the business was bought by William Dixon and production was underway once more. It was to be a short lived rekindling, however, and in 1842 the manufacture of iron finally stopped, though coal mining continued at Wilsontown into the middle of the twentieth century.

In the second period of use the iron workers at Wilsontown stumbled on a process that was to revolutionize the industry of iron smelting in the nineteenth century. It is recorded that early in 1828 a leak sprang in the cold water tank used to control the air pressure to the furnace. The cold water had to be replaced, but the only water available was warm — that which had been run through the condensers for the steam engine. This was quite against the established principles for iron work, but to their surprise the furnace managers found that it actually improved the quality of the iron which they produced. William Dixon contracted one James Beaumont Neilson from Glasgow to repair the tank and on his return to Glasgow Neilson filed a patent for the hot blast process. This patent was to make him rich: not only did he gather the credit for the invention; but he also amassed a royalty of one shilling per ton for iron that was produced by his method. He retired a wealthy man, and devoted himself to improvements and good works in Kirkcudbrightshire. The furnaces at Wilsontown were always exempt from this royalty, though Neilson never revealed the origins of his idea (Murray 1958).

Despite the long history of development on the site, the early remains at Wilstontown are extensive and individual elements from the first iron working can still be made out. These include the remains of two blast furnaces, together with a forge and other associated buildings such as coke and lime kilns. The footings of the terraces that housed the workers may be seen and other buildings have been identified as various shops, including the company store, and an inn. In addition, the circular openings of early bell pits cover an extensive area of ground in a recently forested area to the east of the works, together with a reservoir and lades designed to supply water to the works. On the ground it is hard to make out the various humps and bumps that go together to make up this faded industrial landscape, but an aerial photograph helps to reveal it more clearly. It is important to remember that the forestry itself, which now plays such a major part in this landscape, is but a sign of the times — an indication of modern economics and preoccupations.

Kames, Muirkirk: coal mines and tarworks
Ayrshire, NS 693 255
NS62NE 16

The impetus for the tar industry at Kames, in Muirkirk, was the local occurrence of coal to feed the kilns. The remains in the photograph therefore comprise a variety of elements including the old coal shafts, the tar works, the terraced footings of the workers accommodation and the transport system, including tramroads, that linked them all together. As these remains cover an extensive area, but have little upstanding material, an aerial photograph is necessary in order to get an idea of their complexity.

The tar kilns here were built by the British Tar Company in 1786, but they were bought in 1790 by J.L. McAdam. This was an intensive production site: the mine shafts are closely spaced, each with a spoil dump and sometimes with visible remains from the horse-engine platforms that provided winding power. There are also the remains of a complex series of

133

drains that was devised to prevent flooding and which included the diversion of a local burn, the Colt Burn, in order to lead water away from the mines. Over 80 disused shafts have been identified, each slowly returning to nature. By 1856 the mines had gone out of use, though industrial activity including mineral extraction continued in the area.

In the western part of the Muirkirk mineral field, at Nether Wellwood, Ayrshire (*NS 660 252, NS62NE 18*), the old mine shafts have a different appearance. They are more widely spaced and each is surrounded by the remains of a lobate bing, the slag heap of waste material. In some cases the locations of the stances for machinery may still be made out, and there are also the remains of opencast working as well as areas where the underground galleries have subsided. This land has quickly reverted to a more rural atmosphere, but it is not hard to imagine the noise and the dust when the workings were operative.

Wanlockhead: water pressure engine
Dumfriess-shire, NS 870 131
NS81SE 2

Wanlockhead is an area where significant industrial processes have made their mark on the landscape, but it is no longer one of Scotland's industrial centres. Records of mineral extraction in the vicinity go back into the thirteenth century, though it is only in the 1560s that it seems to have become important, and it was always a vulnerable industry. The mines were abandoned for much of the seventeenth century and again between 1834 and 1850. Production all but ceased in 1918 and an attempt to reopen the mines in 1948 was not successful. The main metal to be extracted was lead, though there are records of the associated gold which became, from time to time, more attractive.

135

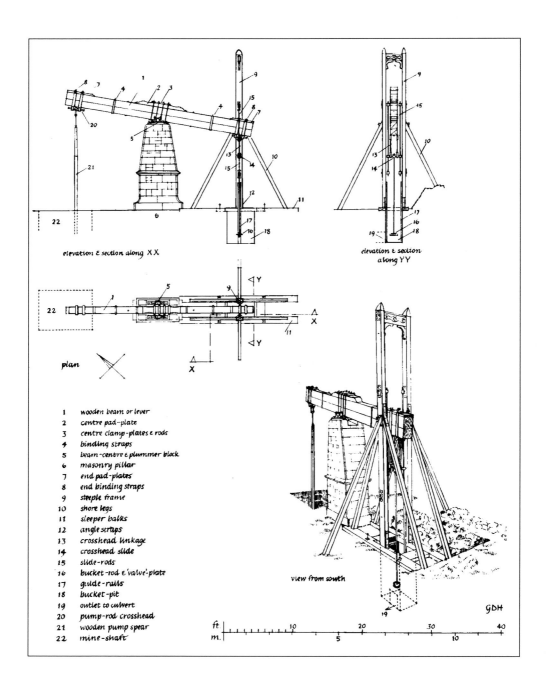

elevation & section along X X

elevation & section
along Y Y

plan

1	wooden beam or lever
2	centre pad-plate
3	centre clamp-plates & rods
4	binding straps
5	beam-centre & plummer block
6	masonry pillar
7	end pad-plates
8	end binding straps
9	steeple frame
10	shore legs
11	sleeper balks
12	angle straps
13	crosshead linkage
14	crosshead slide
15	slide-rods
16	bucket-rod & 'valve'-plate
17	guide-rails
18	bucket-pit
19	outlet to culvert
20	pump-rod crosshead
21	wooden pump spear
22	mine-shaft

view from south

GDH

ft
m.

This beam engine stands on part of the Straightsteps Mine, at the north end of Wanlockhead village. It was built towards the end of the nineteenth century and was used to drain water from nearby abandoned shafts in order to maintain the mine. Although this was a common piece of mining equipment throughout the nineteenth century, this particular engine is believed to be the only one that has survived more-or-less intact. It is a good example of the way in which the human alterations of the countryside do not only involve large buildings or diggings; there is a range of smaller constructions that go together to make up the context of a place.

The engine was operated by water power. The water was piped into a rectangular bucket at one end and the weight of the full bucket caused the beam to fall at that end. When it reached the bottom of the bucket pit, some 1.5m down, the water was released through a flap so that the arm of the beam was lighter thereby causing it to rise. In this way the beam engine would move up and down regularly, thus operating the pumping machinery which was carried on the opposite arm of the beam. The pump is mainly built of wood, strengthened with metal. It has been noted that it is all built to a high standard and that the iron parts were carefully cast with the moving parts held in brass bearings (Hay & Stell, 1986, 136-7).

Today the mining has gone and Wanlockhead has adapted itself to a new, and very different, Scottish industry: tourism. Though the traces of metal extraction have left scars that will take many years to heal, this is once again a rural area of wild beauty. People come here both to learn about the ways of the past, and to enjoy the scenery of the present. Even tourism, however, is a fragile foundation on which to base rural economics and, at the time of writing in late 2000, the future of the carefully developed museum service that seeks to interpret the remains, both above and below the ground, is in jeopardy. Should the service fail it will no doubt provide its own set of archaeological features in time as car parks grass over and interpretative buildings decay. The landscape of tourism will be an important feature for those who seek to understand and interpret Scotland at the turn of the millennium.

West Calder: Five Sisters oil-shale bing
West Lothian, NT 009 640
NT06SW 22

On occasion the scale of archaeological remains is such that they add to the landscape in an impressive way. This is so in West Lothian, where the creation of shale-oil bings — the slag-heaps thrown up from the residues of over 100 years of shale extraction — has added whole new ranges of 'hills' to the sky-line.

The Five Sisters, seen here, near to West Calder, is a substantial bing and has now taken its place as an important feature of the local landscape. The Sisters comprise conical mounds of waste material from the shale-oil industry. The extraction of oil in the area goes back to the 1850s when James Young patented a process to extract it from cannel coal, a rich bituminous coal that occurred locally. The oil was distilled for use in a number of products, and the process was further refined in the 1860s when rich oil-bearing shale deposits were discovered at about the same time as the deposits of cannel coal began to dwindle. In order to extract the oil the shales are heated and oxidised, thus turning them red. This gives the bings their distinctive hue. The material from the Five Sisters bing was processed at the nearby Westwood Oil Works well into the early twentieth century, when it was replaced by other processes.

The shale was heated in retorts in order to extract the oil which could then be distilled and used in various ways. The waste material was then dumped into these characteristic mounds thus ensuring that, even once the remains of the Westwood Oil Works itself were long gone, the bing would remain as a reminder of past industrial glories. With time, the slopes of the mounds start to grass over as vegetation develops, thus drawing them even further back into the 'natural' landscape.

Though they are impressive, not all bings have endured in the same way as the Five Sisters. Material from others has been removed and transported to the shores of the Forth nearby where it has been used to create huge embankments to screen the oil storage tanks at the BP tank farm. As this has been built well within the close confines of Edinburgh, great care has been taken to lessen its environmental impact. The archaeological landscape of the future grows more and more complex as our capacity to make alterations becomes increasingly refined.

Ballachulish: East Laroch slate quarry
Argyll, NN 085 583
NN05NE 9

The landscape of Scotland has provided for a great natural wealth in times past. There was abundant stone for quarrying and diverse minerals to be extracted. Long sea lochs provided easy access to transport and considerable stretches of woodland could be managed to provide charcoal for fuel. Quarrying has long been an important industry, making use of Scotland's varied rocks whose natural properties provided for many different needs. There were hard volcanic rocks: stone from Salisbury Crags in Edinburgh was being sent to London for setts in the late seventeenth century. There was fine, decorative marble, quarried in abundance from Iona and Skye. There were softer limestones and sandstones to be used for building. And there were the great slate deposits of Argyll.

The slate quarries at Ballachulish were founded in 1693. Because of the nature of quarrying, as an extractive industry, the remains of earlier workings are often subsumed in the later workings so that the surviving vestiges of today only reflect a certain phase of activity, usually the most recent. In this way therefore, the workings in the photograph reflect mainly the extraction as it was in 1955 when the East Laroch quarry was finally abandoned.

East Laroch was one of two main quarries at Ballachulish. The slate was quarried from five main seams and its fine quality with few inclusions meant that it played an important role in the Scottish slate industry. In 1793 there were 322 men employed here and the slate was exported overseas to America as well as to England and Ireland. By the start of the twentieth century there were 600 employees, and the production totalled 26 million slates yearly. Throughout the early twentieth century, however, demand and production steadily declined so that the quarry was closed in 1955.

The remains at Ballachulish include the workers' housing, built for 72 families in the eighteenth century, and also a harbour, visible in the background of this photograph, built largely out of the waste from the quarry. The quarry itself, though now flooded, is clearly an impressive archaeological monument and it will be some time before nature can reclaim and redevelop it.

The Dalriadan slate seams of Ballachulish meant that Argyll became the heartland of the slate industry between the seventeenth and the mid-twentieth centuries. There are several other slate quarries locally, including those at Easdale and the spooky remains of the island at Belnahua where the centre of the island has been completely quarried away. Slate quarries on a smaller scale may be visited to the north of the town of Lochgilphead. In many ways, all look as if they were simply abandoned when the workforce left one day: old machinery rusts away and doors bang onto empty, roofless rooms.

Harelawhill: limestone quarries and lime works
Dumfries-shire, NY 427 788
NY47NW 16

Limestone has been an important commodity for much of Scotland's industrial past. Crushed limestone was necessary for road construction, but the material was also used in many processes, such as the smelting of iron. In addition, it could be ground down, and lime, from lime kilns, was particularly valued for agriculture in an age before modern fertilizers and soil treatments.

There are numerous deposits of limestone in Scotland and most have been exploited at some time. In the age before mechanized transport many farms had individual lime kilns which were of vital importance to ensure the fertility of the land. Larger quarries and the processing of lime on a greater scale were elements that developed from the late eighteenth century into the nineteenth century.

The limestone quarries at Harelawhill (see **colour plate 24**) belonged to the Duke of Buccleuch who leased them in the 1770s to an Englishman named Lomax. They produced a particularly pure limestone and work here continued through the nineteenth century. The quarrying at Harelawhill took place on a large scale with the workings driven into the hillside in a manner more akin to a coal mine. Associated with the drift mines here are the remains of various sheds and other buildings from the processing and storage of the material. Though the work at Harelawhill ceased at the end of the nineteenth century, it was reopened twice in the twentieth century: in the 1930s and then in 1947, though neither episode lasted long.

Across the landscape of Scotland many smaller remnants of lime processing are preserved in various states from ruinous farm kilns to overgrown industrial kiln-banks such as those at Blackwoodridge, Dumfries-shire (*NY 243 758, NY27NW 69*). There are three quarries at Blackwoodridge, which make use of four outcrops of two different limestones. Two of these quarries and the kiln-bank in the photograph were already in use when the surveyors from the Ordnance Survey came past, and they included them on their map of 1862. The two arches visible in the undergrowth served a single bowl which is well hidden in the shrubbery and trees behind. There is a second kiln-bank at the other end of the quarries, together with various sheds and machinery stores.

By 1900, however, the main quarries and the kilns at Blackwoodridge were out of use and abandoned. Attention had shifted slightly to the south, where a smaller working had been opened up, though it seems to have been short-lived. Sites such as this are an important reminder of the close integration that once existed between the countryside and small-scale industry.

See **colour plate 23**

Drumbuck: copper mine
Kirkcudbrightshire, NX 582 636
NX56SE 33

The mine at Drumbuck was opened in the early twentieth century, in the years preceding the First World War. The remains of four levels for extraction are spread across the hillside, each with their own spoil tips. The associated ruins include a brick-built magazine for the storage of charges, a concrete base for winding gear, and a shuttered concrete tank which was probably used for settling.

The adits lead horizontally into the hillside. Today they are flooded, though the remains of metal rails may be seen to lead into the galleries. This is a typical example of how the rural landscape can hide even apparently highly wasteful industrialized remains. In effect, however, the mines were not in operation for long here and they never produced large quantities of ore. The raw material was crushed and processed on site, but the inefficiency of the machinery involved meant that much of the ore was never recovered.

The mine at Drumbuck is typical of many small-scale extraction sites that have existed in Scotland over the millennia. The landscape of Scotland is rich in many minerals, though most do not exist in the quantities that would make modern working economic. Past industry did not require the same high input of finance and effort so that at various times many different materials have been extracted, and all of these workings have left their mark, though many now blend in to the countryside.

6 CROSSING THE LANDSCAPE: TRANSPORT AND BOUNDARIES

This chapter looks at two basic human traits. People are restless creatures, and they work hard to know and divide their world. Ever since the first exploratory groups made their way here as conditions improved at the end of the Ice Age, movement has been central to life in Scotland. We do not know how the first settlers perceived the landscape in which they lived, but we do know that separate parts of it were good for different things and they would have been well aware of that. We know little of these early settlers for they left little trace behind them and what they did leave has been subject to the ensuing millennia of development. Their tracks and routeways have long since disappeared under the feet of subsequent generations. With time, however, as the routes became more formalized they made their own mark on the land. This effect has been vastly exaggerated in recent centuries with the development of transport systems that need physical paths to follow. The motorways and railway lines of today are but the recent manifestations of a process that has been going on for centuries (the Innocent Railway in Edinburgh).

Extant ancient routeways are therefore relatively few in Scotland as so many lie buried beneath later roads. Sites like the clapper bridge at Clynelish give clues as to the presence of earlier elements to a modern route. The military roads of the Romans (Dolphinton), and later on of the Government troops of the eighteenth century (Coupar Angus), provide rare examples of surviving sections of ancient road. They usually survive where they did not have to bow to the needs of modern transport, such as for gentle gradients. In other places once well-used routes are no longer needed and have been fossilized into the landscape (Hill of Drimmie and Loch Ard).

Further hints to transport are given by the entrance to Dunadd which looks out across the meeting place of sea-going traffic with land traffic. Though today we rely on land-based transport, this is a recent phenomenon. The importance of boats is emphasized by the landing place at Dùn an Rubha Bhuide on Islay, and by the graffiti drawings of ships at Kilchattan on Luing.

As populations grew so did the need for resources, whether land or materials. Thus it became important for separate groups to identify their lands and, through their common ancestry, their rights to be there. Boundaries of different types became important. It is hard to see the divisions of the early inhabitants of the land: they concentrated on natural features, many of which may have had ritual associations with the shared history of the group. With time, however, the boundaries that crossed the land became more visible and physical reminders took their place. Both Scots' Dike and Crink Law are good examples of this, though on very different scales. Scots' Dike was the physical manifestation of a

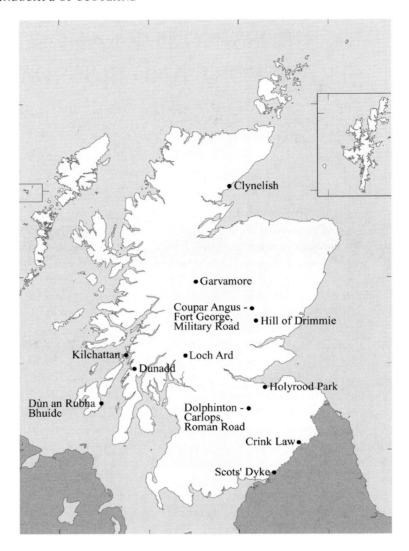

political situation: the general national uncertainties of the early sixteenth century. Crink Law is a more local affair, rooted today in mystery. We do not know whether it owes its origins to the need for political definition, to the interests of local landowners, or to the necessary division of cultivated land from grazing. It is a good example of how the remains of archaeology do not necessarily reflect the status of their originators.

Dùn an Rubha Bhuidhe, Islay: boat landing
Islay, NR 466 540
NR45SE 6

The sea was of immeasurable importance to the early inhabitants of Scotland because it provided both a method of transport and a resource to be harvested. It is hard for us today to see the country from the point of view of its contact with the sea, but this is a side to life that has only recently been lost, with the rise of wheeled transport and the technology to tame the land under a network of roads and railways. The maritime viewpoint is important, however, for it completely alters the perception of our geography: without good roads and with a reliance on water for transport, places that are now remote become easily accessible, while others that are currently at the heart of things become quite difficult, and therefore slow, of access.

It is perhaps surprising that so little remains as a physical record of the early viewpoint. In many cases the remains have long gone, but there are examples that are still there but have been given little attention. At Dùn an Rubha Bhuidhe in Islay there is a small Promontory Fort protected by a massive wall up to 4m thick and still standing to over 1m high. Little other detail survives of the internal arrangements and nature of this site, which was one of many similar sites built to shelter the small local communities in the years between 500 BC and AD 500. At Dùn an Rubha Bhuidhe, however, there is an

151

added detail outside the fort which is the survival of a small cleared landing place among the rocks of the foreshore.

The seaborne connections of the community here would have been particularly important. Their own small galley pulled into the landing to offload goods and visitors and take on-board materials to be traded. From here their men would set out to support the heads of the wider community in disputes which might sometimes lead to warfare. Not all came back and those left at home would come here to receive the bad news — bodies, or mementos, of their loved ones. The landing saw both local boats and visiting boats. It sheltered the small fishing boats of those who lived in the fort and surrounding lands and it housed the larger longboats of passing merchants and potentates. It may even have provided the first step ashore when missionaries came from across the water to spread the word of God.

We do not know the precise date when the promontory fort of Dùn an Rubha Bhuidhe was occupied. We have no archaeological details of those who cleared the rocks to make way for the boats to approach the shore. But their work has survived and through it they were linked in to the arteries of sea that have supported life in the West of Scotland over many millennia.

Dolphinton — Carlops: Roman road
Lanarkshire/Midlothian, NT 109 473 — NT 161 561
NT14NW 39

The Roman army is well known for one of its contributions to life in Britain: transport and communications in Roman-dominated parts of the country and the construction of the straight, well-made, road. Many of these roads have been subsumed into the modern transport system and, if they survive at all, they now lie buried beneath tons of road metal and ballast. In some cases, however, the routeways favoured by the Romans deviate from those in modern use, and these may often be seen as levelled grassy thoroughfares which cross the land today.

The road from Dolphinton to Carlops contains stretches of both type of preservation. This was a major Roman routeway that is thought to have led from the Borders up to the fort at Inveresk on the eastern fringes of Edinburgh. The modern communications follow this same route and for long stretches of the way the position of the Roman road is well buried below the present tarmac. In other places, however, where it lies to one side or the other, it is visible on the surface. Elsewhere, lengths of previously lost road have been recorded as cropmarks in aerial photographs. In this photograph, the remains of the road are clearly visible as they rise up over the hillside.

Road engineering was a skilled matter in the Roman Empire. The routes were carefully surveyed and the road itself was levelled and cambered where necessary. Strength was provided by rough ballast with a stone metalled surface laid over the top. There were ditches on either side, with culverts for drainage as necessary. It is hardly surprising that these roads have left their mark on the land after so much time, but it is also a measure of their quality that so many have survived for so long as the basis of later communications.

Dunadd: entrance to the fort
Argyll, NR 836 935
NR89SW 1

The rock on which the Early Historic fort of Dunadd sits may not be particularly high, but Dunadd is surely one of the most impressive forts in Scotland. Many features here combine to provide an extraordinary sense of place, but one of the most emotive things for the modern visitor must be the entrance through a narrow rocky defile where one treads precisely the same path as the community who lived here in the sixth to ninth centuries AD.

Large stretches of fortified walling have survived at Dunadd and it is possible to see how the builders of the fort made use of the natural contours of the hill to construct a series of interior settings, each placed higher than the last. The ascending importance of each was emphasized and archaeologists generally assume that access would have been increasingly restricted as one neared the centre. Only the privileged were allowed to visit the buildings at the top. The main entrance, however, was accessible to all, though it is nonetheless impressive as it makes its way through a deep natural cut in the rocks. In the past this natural grandeur would have been emphasized by stone and timber fortifications rising up above the rocks, and perhaps with the use of colour. Even today it is a most theatrical setting. Kings and warriors have passed through this entrance, to fight and to dominate by negotiation; traders have passed through to ply their wares; ordinary people have passed through as they went about their everyday lives — setting out for the fields to work, leaving for and returning from journeys, visiting family, merely wandering. When we pass between the rocks it is hard not to hear the ghosts of past voices echoing around us.

Dunadd is a very personal site for it is one of the first archaeological sites to appear in the literature. We can give names to some of the people who climbed the hill, and we know of some of the things that they were doing here. Twice the fort is recorded as under siege. Once in AD 683, and again in AD 736, when it was besieged by Aengus, son of Fergus, King of the Picts. Rivalry between the Pictish Kingdom and that of the Scots is well known and scholars now identify Dunadd as one of the centres of power of the kingdom of the Scots. It would have made an important prize. Aengus was eventually successful and it is recorded that he took two important Scottish prisoners here — Donngal and Feradach — who have been identified as leading members of the local aristocracy. Warfare such as this inevitably leads to the rise of new personalities and influences, and there are carvings within the higher citadel which seem to have a Pictish aspect. These have been suggested as dating to the inauguration of a new king after the fall of the fort.

It is important to remember, however, that life at Dunadd was not all about fighting. Excavations at the site have yielded evidence that life for some in the fort had its comforts. Fine-quality metal goods were made here — there were skilled jewellers with a local market who could afford to buy their precious brooches and pins. Luxury goods were imported from across Europe. There are indications that some of the inhabitants were literate, and Christianity may have been practiced here. This is backed up by a text which describes how in the sixth century AD the saint Columba came to one of the communities in this area, described as 'the chief place' and met with sailors from Gaul (in Adomnan's *Life of Columba)*. This meeting has been identified as taking place at Dunadd. If this is so, Columba also would have made his way through the imposing entrance to the fort as he arrived for his ministry.

See **colour plate 24**

Kilchattan, Luing: ship graffiti
Argyll, NM 744 090
NM70NW 2

The roofless ruins of the twelfth-century church of Kilchattan stand within its burial ground at the centre of the island of Luing. It is a simple, rectangular building that seems to have gone out of use in the early eighteenth century when a new church was built and dedicated.

On the surface the ruins appear unremarkable, but they are interesting because of the presence of graffiti incised on the walls. There is no precise date for this graffiti, but it is thought to be pre-Reformation at least. Not only does the graffiti remind us of the enduring nature of the human character — we still seek to adorn and leave a message in blank spaces — but the graffiti also provides us with a unique insight into very personal concerns. The artist knew that the drawing would be covered with plaster, and this art was not designed for public show. It is more in the nature of a letter from the past.

The subject matter of the fragment pictured here is clearly the sea. At least three vessels can be seen: the long, masted, wooden birlinns that once graced the seaways of the Western Isles. One is much larger than the others, and the keen eye may even detect a hint of its occupants ranged along the superstructure. There is at least one anchor, and a shoal of fish seem to be swimming off to the left.

The importance of the sea in the past can hardly be overemphasized. In the days before motorized vehicles, water transport was the easiest way in which to move around. The west coast of Scotland, with its long inlets and sheltered passages between islands, provided a natural motorway for the time. The waters could be treacherous, and navigation was a skilled matter, but relatively easy access was afforded to both the coastlands and, via the sea lochs, well into the heartlands. Goods as well as people could be moved around and, at the same time, the sea could be harvested to provide a rich supply of foodstuffs and other things. Boats like these were used both for everyday tasks and to transport larger groups of people when local feuding lead to some intense sea battles. The birlinns would have made an impressive sight as they cruised between the islands.

We can never know the precise thoughts that lead the graffiti artist of some 500 years ago to incise this scene on the unplastered stones of Kilchattan church. But we can be sure of the importance of their subject matter. Building and sailing a birlinn were highly skilled tasks, and maintaining the boats was vital. Their well-being lay right at the heart of the community.

See colour plate 25

Scots' Dike: national boundary
Dumfries-shire, NY 387 731
NY37SE 6

In 1552 the western reaches of the border between Scotland and England were marked by an earthwork bank that stretched between the River Sark and the River Esk. Although there were efforts to destroy it in the early years of the twentieth century, the bank has survived in the Scotsdike Plantation and today it stands to a height of 0.8m. Slight ditches survive on either side of the bank, though the carved stones that stood at either end of the dike, bearing the royal arms of Scotland and England, have long since disappeared.

The boundary dike was built in the reign of Mary, known as Mary Queen of Scots. At the time she was only 10 years old and living in France. Scotland was under the regency of her mother, Mary of Guise, though she also lived in France. This was a time of great unrest with both political and religious turmoil at home in Scotland. The country stood as a key player in the complex sequence of jostling for power between England and France, but it did not do her any good. Repeated defeats by the English — at Flodden in 1513 and Solway Moss in 1542 — were symptomatic of a general unease in the country, and various means of fortification such as the building of the Flodden Wall around Edinburgh had already taken place. Different factions competed for political influence across the country. At the same time, repeated challenges to the Church were taking hold across Europe and their influence spread with surprising rapidity. The effect in Scotland was to add another layer to the general undermining of the political foundations of society. Men such as John Knox were powerful influences on a people who had already had to face many different uncertainties to the previously established order of life.

It was against this background that the Scots' Dike was built. Strategically, the Solway had always been a weak point on the Border, and the dike lay just at the point where the Border ran inland from the coast. Not surprisingly, the frontier had been drawn up very much along natural features, running first up the River Sark and then along the Esk, but there was a point between the two rivers where a stretch of some 5km ran over land. Here, the dike was built. It still marks the boundary today, and it is preserved for almost its entire length within a forestry plantation.

In Britain today we are unused to political boundaries, though they have been treated with much more importance at different times in the past, as the successive monuments of Hadrian's Wall, the Antonine Wall, and the Scots' Dike show. It is surprising to us, therefore, to realise that this thin stretch of woodland running across the gentle farmlands of Dumfries-shire marks out an ancient boundary, and one the life of which has not yet, seemingly, come to an end.

Hill of Drimmie: braided trackways
Perthshire, NO 191 494
NO14NE 62

Not all roads were as well built as the Roman roads and the later military roads of General Wade. Metalled surfaces were unknown on most routeways and in times of wet weather they must have turned into quagmires. Furthermore, most roads were not the results of careful survey and planning — they came about through the common use of a particular track as the best way to get from A to B. In this way, repeated use wore out a hollow way which took the brunt of the traffic, though on occasion, perhaps when the mud got particularly bad, travellers would move to one side or another to facilitate their journey. Many hollow ways were subsequently metalled over and incorporated into the roads and farm lanes that criss-cross the countryside, but some fell out of use and these have been fossilized into the face of the land.

Well-used trackways of this nature can be seen at Hill of Drimmie in Perthshire where the passage of traffic over many centuries has worn down a series of hollow ways. As each in turn became impassable, through mud or narrowness and depth, another was formed to the side, so that over the years a broad band of trackways developed. These may be seen clearly in the aerial photograph, though from below it is hard to discern the extent of ground which they cover. Trackways like this may sometimes be dated by association, with particular sites such as an Iron Age fort or a medieval settlement, but often it is hard to assign a particular period to their use. It is likely, of course, that many routes remained in use over many, many years: the amount and extent of use may in part be gauged by the depth of wear. Many of these routes became particularly important to the drovers who took their great herds of cattle south for the market, and this went on right through the nineteenth century.

Though it is hard to gauge the extent of an old road from the ground, they can also make interesting archaeological sites. In Loch Ard forest in Stirlingshire (*NN 401 089, NN40NW 3*) an old road runs for a distance of some 3km to one side of the present public road. It makes an evocative sight as it runs through the trees, though there are sections where it is not so clear, especially where the drainage has gone and where timbers have been felled across the track. It is a well-built road that originally had culverts to provide drainage and small bridges, most of which have now gone. This road is likely to date from the eighteenth or nineteenth centuries and it may have been built as a Statute Labour Road using a local workforce.

Bridges and drainage were obviously important to a road whether it was carefully laid out and built as a designed project or whether it was a more local affair. The clapper bridge was a simple form of low bridge. The name derives from the Latin '*claperius*', which means a pile of stones, and these are small stone bridges, ideally built of long

thin slabs laid across stone piers to provide a surface. The particular type of slab can vary according to the properties of the locally available stone. Clapper bridges were popular in the medieval period, though they continued in use in later times, particularly in rural areas. They were built throughout Britain, and a few survive, to be seen to one side of the modern roadway, marking out the line of a previous road. At Brora, Clynelish (*Sutherland, NC 894 055, NC80NE 42*) a small clapper bridge has been recorded, though much obscured by vegetation.

Crink Law: boundary
Roxburghshire, NT 660 081
NT60NE 68

Boundaries are made for many different reasons. They may denote international frontiers, the marches of a particular lord, the edge of private land, or a change in cultivation practices. Many survive with no written record to tell of their making.

The boundary at Crink Law is one of the latter. Today it survives as a shallow ditch with a low bank on either side and it is hard to make it out in the photograph, being visible where the bank runs from the foreground into the middle distance. Archaeologists often have to work with minimal remains such as this. They learn to recognize the coarse humps and bumps that signify past activity. There are often other clues, however, and at Crink Law a clear differentiation may be seen in the vegetation across the surface of the boundary. While bog cotton is obviously very suited to the prevailing damp conditions of the area, the low banks on either side of the boundary ditch are clearly somewhat better drained and drier so that the boundary shows up as a swathe of green grass against the white-spotted background. Differentiation such as this is vital to the archaeologist who works with a whole suite of factors when identifying and examining sites in the field.

Although it does not look like much today, the boundary was clearly more significant in the past. Not only have there been several centuries for the definition of the banks and ditch to blur with erosion and silting, but there may have been other aspects to it that have long since gone. Many boundaries such as this would have had thorn hedges or other shrubs along their length to provide a substantial and effective deterrent to those (whether human or animal) who wished to cross it.

The land here today is largely uncultivated, clearly lying at the limits of modern agriculture, but it was not always so in the past. The Crink Law boundary crosses an archaeological landscape which comprises the remains of rig and furrow cultivation, as well as traces of a farmstead and various other buildings and enclosures. This has been, even if only for short spells of time, fertile farmland. As the rig and furrow seems to skirt the boundary, it is likely that the boundary is earlier than this latest phase of cultivation. This theory is supported by the fact that other banks, more closely associated with the cultivation remains, clearly cross it. It seems likely that the Crink Law boundary had gone out of use by the time that cultivation once more stretched up to tame the upper slopes.

Why was the Crink Law boundary built? We have no certain answer — but given that it is sited right at the heart of the long contested and unstable Border country between England and Scotland a whole host of possible reasons rear their heads.

Coupar Angus — Fort George: military road
Perthshire, NO 142 626
NO16SW 159

In the early eighteenth century the Government in London was aware of the need for good communications throughout the Highlands if it was to control them effectively. This need became even more apparent with the uprising of 1715, and in the 1720s General George Wade was sent north to look into the situation in the Highlands and to make a start on control by building a network of roads and bridges.

Wade built over 250 miles of roads, many of which have been subsumed into modern roads and lost to sight. At this stretch in Perthshire, however, Wade's military road may be seen leaving the course of the modern road which skirts the hill across which Wade drove his road. Like his Roman predecessors Wade tended to ignore the difficulties presented by the Scottish landscape so that stretches of his road system follow steep inclines that would present problems for modern vehicles.

164

Of course the nature of the Scottish landscape meant that Wade had also to become something of a bridge builder. At Garvamore in Inverness-shire (*NN 521 947, NN59SW 2*) the military road between Fort Augustus and the barracks at Ruthven had to cross the Spey, a river width of some 50m. To do this a double-arched bridge was designed, making use of a bed of rock that jutted out of the river. This was the first double-arched bridge that Wade built and it was completed in 1732. The roadway is 3m wide, and is enclosed by high parapets.

Wade worked in the Highlands for 11 years. His road system transformed communications there. It was, ironically, so successful that in 1745 the rebellious Jacobite army used his roads to avoid the government forces under Sir John Cope and to speed its march south.

The roads led to other building and developments. Increased traffic opened the way for the spread of goods and ideas and it also meant that there was an increased demand for accommodation along the way. Near to the bridge at Garvamore is a large two-storey building, which was built around 1740 and used by both soldiers and civilians overnight when they crossed the Corrieyairack Pass. In later years it was used by the drovers as they took their cattle south to the markets and it has also been used as a keeper's house.

See **colour plate 26**

Edinburgh, Holyrood Park: the Innocent Railway
Midlothian, NT 286 720
NT27SE 553

The romantically named Innocent Railway was built in 1831. It ran from Dalkeith to Edinburgh and carried coal from the mines of Midlothian into the city for domestic use. The railway closed down in the 1960s, and today the track is used as a cycle path and public walkway. It just clips the Royal Park of Holyrood and is a popular thoroughfare. For most of its length it now boasts a modern surface, but occasionally a glimpse of the old sleepers breaks through, as here at the Braid Burn Bridge on Duddingston Road West. It is a good example of how even within a city there are layers of the past to be seen, and they usually show how much things have changed.

Though in later years the trains of the Innocent Railway were pulled by steam engines, originally the trucks were horse drawn and this lead to its peculiar name. The nickname arose because of the supposed dangers of the newfangled steam trains as opposed to the apparent safety of the horse! The horse-drawn railway had an excellent safety record and Edinburgh publisher Dr Robert Chambers wrote of 'the innocence of the railway'. It was to be a phrase which stuck.

The Innocent Railway was designed by a well-known Edinburgh engineer, James Jardine, and it was quite a feat of construction. The rails ran along a flat track at the side of Duddingston Loch and it included a stone tunnel, a cast-iron bridge, and a timber viaduct. Although originally designed for freight, local people soon took to riding in the wagons and it became very popular with passengers. The railway company quickly added passenger carriages converted from ordinary road coaches, and in 1832 a station was opened at St Leonards in the city. The station had a chequered history, with a series of closures and reopenings, but the railway was popular well into the twentieth century.

7 CEREMONY AND RELIGION
IN THE LANDSCAPE

This chapter was one of the most challenging. All too often ceremony and ritual have been the grey boxes into which archaeological problems have been dropped. At the same time, the rigid separation that is perceived by most Scots between their 'domestic' lives and any religious activity is a modern construct. There are still sections of society for whom religious observance is an everyday matter— and we all have our own little 'rituals'. These should show us that the secular side of life is not an entity that can be clearly separated from a deeper meaning.

Our interpretations of the world of the past are often influenced by our feelings about the world of the present. It can be very difficult to picture the role played by religious beliefs in the actions of the early inhabitants of Scotland. Of course, for the first 8000 years there are no written texts so that we are merely making an educated guess when we discuss the role of a particular site or suite of sites. We base our work on artefactual and other evidence, and we use ethnographic examples of similar sites to broaden our interpretations, but they are still guesses.

Nevertheless, there are some types of site where ceremony appears to dominate. These include the circular earthen henge sites (Wormy Hillock and North Mains). Sites like this were often altered during their active life. As the needs of the community changed and alterations in ceremony were developed, so the sites were adapted to provide for this. Some of the changes seem to have included major modifications to ritual and focus, while others were more minor. Just as the great cathedrals and minsters of today have constantly changed since the process of building them began, the ceremonial sites of the past were rarely left alone for long and this is reflected in the archaeological remains.

Ceremonial activity in the third and fourth millennia BC seems to have been a group effort. These sites were designed to emphasize the links between the community and their landscape. This included not only the physical land where they hunted and farmed, but also the celestial landscape that ruled the seasons, weather, and even day and night. Many of the sites have been shown to have particular links to the movement of the sun, moon or stars, and in this way people could make sense of world in which they lived. Perhaps they sought to control it; perhaps they were content to live by its agenda — we can never know. These sites appeal to us because of their mystery and enigma. What are we to make of the stone rows of the north, like the site at Battle Moss? The precise lay out of the stones, and the effort that has gone into their collection, transportation and erection, are clear. They provide a sense of the importance of the site for the ancient community and it is not hard to imagine the activity, colour and music as people celebrated here. But what were they doing?

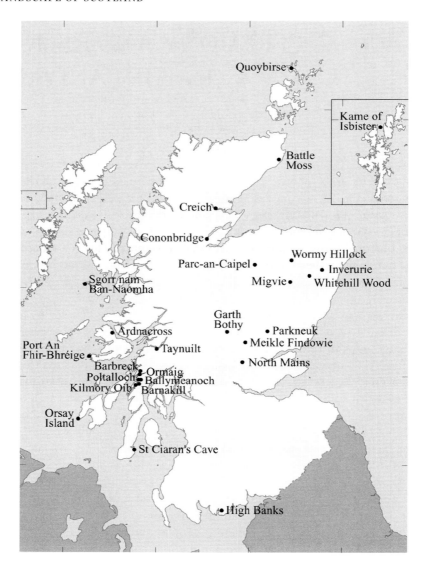

About 4000 years ago there was a sudden shift in emphasis. The scale of sites changes and the area available for ceremony often seems to contract. There was much alteration of existing sites (Ballymeanoch). Elsewhere, new monuments were built (Parkneuk). These innovations reflect considerable changes that may, in turn, have been based on a shift in religious belief. At the same time there appear swathes of pecked cup and ring marks, painstakingly worked across sheets of native rock (Poltalloch); but what did they mean? They are often in spectacular locations, but there are few clues as to their purpose. Cup and ring marks were also made on individual stones, and they appear on standing stones (Ballymeanoch) as well as on stones that have been built into tombs and stone circles. Some sort of symbolic, probably ritual, significance seems clear (and many have been put forward), but they remain one of the mysteries of the Stone Age.

The link between religious belief and art is further explored by the Pictish symbol stone from Inverurie. Though much more recent than the rock art of the Bronze Age, the precise meaning and use of the Pictish symbols have long since been lost. Pictish art had a clear duality which linked images of the everyday world with ceremony and religion. It also provides an important connection with a world which is more familiar today. While many Pictish stones were set up in the years preceding the widespread adoption of Christianity, others combine 'new' Christian motifs with traditional Pictish motifs (Migvie).

Christianity brought with it its own suite of remains. Simple caves (St Ciaran's in Campbelltown), tiny individual sites such as crosses and wells (Kilmory Oib, Barnakill, Creich), and more complex built sites (Sgorr nom Ban-Naomha in Canna), all demonstrate the way in which Christianity lay at the heart of communities right across Scotland. The early church has left its mark on the land. Even here there are still mysteries, like the cairns of Port an Fhir-Bhréige in Iona.

There is one final image: that of the memorial at Taynuilt. This is a reflection of the start of the loosening of the hold of Christianity. The rise of the cult of the hero has also been an important development of the last two centuries, fueled in recent decades by the impact of a sophisticated mass media. What sites would form the ceremonial monuments of today? Football stadiums; leisure complexes; shopping malls; or airports — we could all put forward candidates. While we still have overtly religious buildings, the meaning and place of religion within the community are once again shifting. Despite the standardizing effects of the global media, the society in which we live has fragmented and we now have access to an unprecedented variety of ways in which to express our need for a deeper meaning to life.

Wormy Hillock: henge
Aberdeenshire, NJ 449 307
NJ43SW 1

The external bank and internal platform of the small ceremonial site in **colour plate 27** show up clearly with their differential vegetation cover, but most henge sites today are very denuded and hard to spot on the ground. Henges date to the Neolithic, some 5000 years ago, and they are generally thought to have been the precursors of many stone circles. In some places there is a direct relationship, where a stone circle can be shown to have been built inside a pre-existing henge site, as at Stenness in Orkney.

We can never be sure exactly what took place at henge sites, but they were ceremonial centres carefully designed to control community participation and link into the surrounding landscape. Henges are defined by their external banks, some of which were of considerable size. The bank surrounds a circular ditch inside which a level platform was created. Excavation has revealed that, in some cases, there were timber settings on the platform,

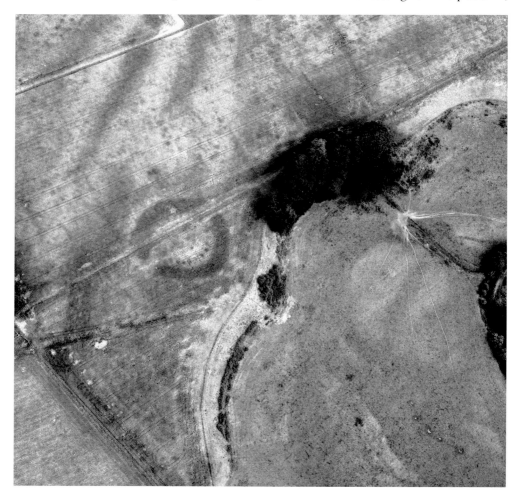

usually circles of massive posts, together with other features and sometimes hearth sites. These structures were sometimes altered and added to during the life of the henge and, as noted above, in later years some were superseded by circles of stone.

The rites that took place at a henge were no doubt diverse, but they seem to have included some that were related to the disposal of the dead, perhaps prior to their being settled into a tomb. As such it has been noted that henges mark a change away from the focus of those rites at the tomb itself. They represent the broadening out of participation away from the immediate community of the dead person at the tomb to wider society at a more central place. Many henges are very large indeed, though others such as that at Wormy Hillock remind us of the ongoing importance of small, stable communities. The finds from henge excavations include fragments of finely decorated pottery, as well as a range of stone tools, and a nice touch is provided by some of the pottery from a henge at Balfarg Riding School in Fife where traces of henbane, a powerful hallucinogen, were recovered. We rarely get a glimpse of the colour of ceremony in prehistoric life, but it is not hard to imagine how natural elements such as this would be incorporated into something as important as relations with the ancestors and the gods.

Wormy Hillock was therefore an important place for the local Neolithic community long before the establishment of the forestry that surrounds it in the photograph. Other henges show up only as aerial photographs, as at North Mains, Strathallan (Perthshire, *NN928 162; NN91NW 18*), where the upstanding remains were long since lost to ploughing. Just rarely, however, modern development may take account of a site, as at Cononbridge, Ross and Cromarty (*NH 542 550; NH55NW 1*), where a probable henge site has been allocated its own plot along a street at the edge of town. This forms a nice demarcation of the modern urban landscape to include our prehistoric ancestors.

See **colour plates 27 & 28**

Quoybirse: standing stone
Westray, Orkney, HY 444 471
HY44NW 5

Standing stones were a well-established element of the prehistoric ceremonial traditions. They were used in particular to mark out sites and places of ritual significance in the landscape. It is clear that, in this, they served a variety of functions. In some cases an individual stone was sufficient; in other cases settings of several stones, varying from the simple to the highly complex, were necessary. Many stones also served to channel and

guide ceremonial activities in addition to their function as markers of place, in much the same way that churches have long been used.

The spectacular standing stone at Quoybirse stands by itself and the significance of the spot has long been forgotten since it was erected some 4000 years ago. Stone is an enduring aspect of the landscape, however, as clearly illustrated by the cottage in the rear where stone has served not only as a building material but also for the roof. Orkney and Caithness are unusual in having local stone that splits naturally into rectangular slabs and this has long been made use of, for both ritual and for other more mundane purposes.

The stone setting at Barbreck, Argyll (*NM 831 064, NM80NW 19*) differs from Quoybirse in that it comprises several stones. These stones may be divided into at least two groups. The first has two stones, and the other (pictured) stands in a plantation some 100m away. This group comprises five stones of which one is much larger than the other four. It is hard to imagine this setting in its original landscape for it is unlikely that the immediate surroundings of the stones would have been so densely wooded when they were in use. Research has been done at Barbreck to establish whether it is likely that these settings had any astronomical significance with the night sky 4000 years ago, but no clear matches were found. Neither was it possible to match them with obvious notches or landscape markers on the horizon. It is recorded, however, that in the nineteenth century stones were removed to clear the site at Barbreck, in order to build a house, so it is possible that the settings do not survive in their entirety. This was obviously a place of some significance in prehistory because there are also the remains of a cairn as well as a large burial cist, all within a short distance of each other.

of stone monuments known as Recumbent Stone Circles. These are confined to north-east Scotland. In each circle there is one, usually massive, elongated boulder on its side, usually with flanking pillars, surrounded by the other stones of the circle. Recumbent Stone Circles were generally set onto hill terraces, towards the summit of a slope, where clear views both down across the cultivated clearings of the wooded landscape and up into the heights would have been important. The forested setting of the photograph, though romantic to our eyes today, would not have been considered appropriate by the builders of this site some 4500 years ago. The recumbent stones were particularly important — they were often of a different material to the rest, sometimes of more exotic rock. They were set so that to the observer the moon would appear to sink and roll across them as it crossed the night sky at particular times of the year. This must have been a spectacular sight.

The importance of the visual aspects of these sites is emphasized by the use of colour in the stones. At Whitehill Wood the pillars are made of a reddish porphyritic stone that must have been dragged some distance to the spur on which the site sits. At other sites stones of contrasting colours have been set together, and this feature is being recognised increasingly elsewhere. We are only just beginning to open our eyes to the richness of perception that came into play in the past.

Battle Moss, Loch of Yarrows: stone rows
Caithness, ND 312 440
ND34SW 22

These enigmatic rows of stone belong to the Early Bronze Age some 4000 years ago. The site has suffered some damage since it was surveyed by Dryden in 1871, but it is still an impressive monument. The precise reasons why our ancestors collected, laid out and carefully set upright these rows of stone have been lost, but they made a good job of it — many of the stones are still in their original positions.

Stone rows are a relatively rare type of site, confined to Caithness and Sutherland in the north of Scotland, and not even common in that area. The only other part of Britain with a similar type of site is Dartmoor, though other sites are known in Europe, particularly in Brittany. The Scottish rows are composed of small stone slabs set on end in carefully laid out lines. There are eight rows at Battle Moss, of which the longest runs for some 40m. They were built on gently-sloping hillsides and are often associated with cairns or other monuments situated on the slopes above them. At Battle Moss a number of chambered cairns and also standing stones still survive on the hill to the south of the site. One suggestion relating to their function is that they may have served as markers, setting out religious ground and leading the eye, if not the observer in body, to a specific site or burial. Other suggested functions involve more complex arguments relating to astronomical and celestial observations and, of course, the two may have been combined. It has often been said that archaeologists are all too ready to ascribe the function of 'ritual' to anything that they do not understand, and this can certainly be true, but the siting and associations of the stone rows do suggest that here we have a series of truly ritual monuments.

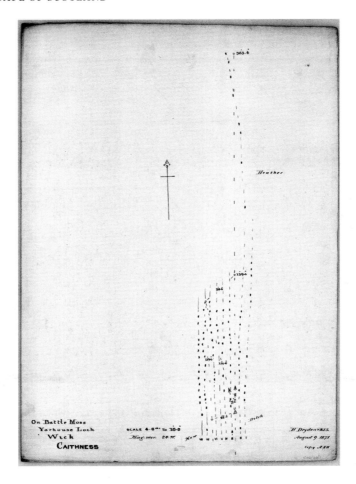

Whatever their purpose, these are evocative sites. Even today the landscape around them seems to be of a special character, often with a particular balance between earth and sky. Covering as they do a greater surface area, but in a more gentle way, than many prehistoric sites, they are a reminder that it was the whole of the landscape (and indeed skyscape) which was important in the past.

Ardnacross: cairns and standing stones
Mull, NM 541 491
NM54NW 3

In many ways the surviving monuments give a very fragmentary record of the past. One problem is that we tend to regard them in isolation, though it is obvious that they must have operated in conjunction with other structures to make a living landscape. Sadly, in many cases the landscape of today is so different from that of the past (at any period) that it is hard to piece together a picture of how things were. Ardnacross, however, is one of the rare places where it is possible to look at several sites together and place them within a wider setting.

The immediate vicinity of this photograph contains a compact series of stone settings that apparently worked together to enhance the ritual aspects of life in the Bronze Age, some 4000 years ago. Further afield, but still within the general neighbourhood, the RCAHMS surveyors have recorded other sites of the same period that emphasize the apparently religious significance of this landscape in prehistory.

The immediate stone settings comprise three kerb cairns, which were probably originally associated with burials, flanked to the north and south by alignments of three standing stones. A recent archaeological project, including some excavation, has been assessing this site, in particular the stone rows, in order to test the hypothesis that the rows were aligned on prominent landscape features or astronomical events. Our attempts to understand the many stone circles and settings that were built in Scotland at this time have long concentrated on the astronomical and celestial features that mark the passing

181

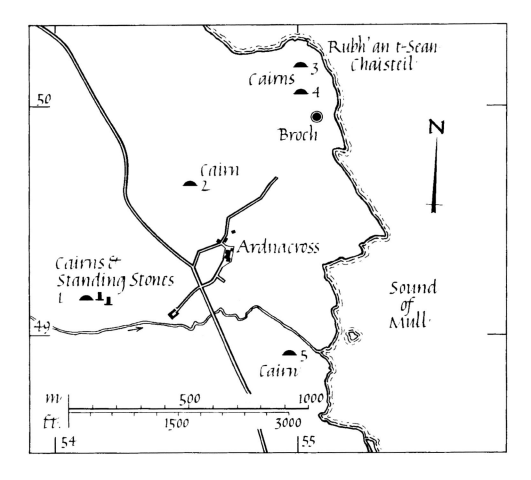

of the seasons, years and even longer periods. This sort of measurement must have been of great importance to a society that relied on planting and on the harvest for much of its economic resource base. As the sun dipped behind a particular hill, or as the moon touched the top of a stone row, people would know that the time had come to start the seasonal round once more. It is difficult, however, to be certain about our interpretation of these events. Ironically, the dramatic Scottish landscape provides a plethora of possible summits or cols that may be aligned with individual stones or settings, while astronomical events have not, of course, remained static over the millennia. It is possible, however, with advanced statistical analysis and modern computers to look with more certainty at possible alignments.

At Ardnacross, excavation has revealed that this was a cultivated landscape prior to the erection of the monuments. Ard marks from early ploughing covered the surface of the ground around the southern stone row and carbonised cereal grains were recovered. It also seems that both rows of stones were deliberately destroyed, but in a very controlled way: the end stones of each row were pushed over into pits and the central stones left standing. In the northern row this stone later fell of its own accord. The final analysis of

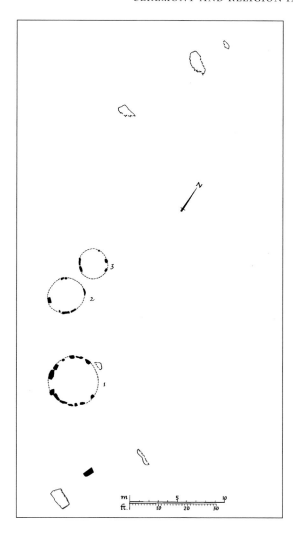

the astronomical significance of this site has yet to be published, but it is hard not to be impressed by the landscape setting within which the prehistoric builders were working. Even today the views are spectacular.

Parkneuk: stone circle
Perthshire, NO 195 514
NO15SE 5

Parkneuk is a good example of a type of small stone circle known as a 'Four Poster' from the four prominent stones. This type of circle is particularly common at the edges of the fertile farmlands as in north-east Perthshire, and the location of Parkneuk typifies this. Though it may seem something of a misnomer to class such a rectangular monument as a 'circle' their ancestry has been traced through small settings of stones back to the Recumbent Stone Circles of Aberdeenshire.

Four Posters seem to have been in use during the Bronze Age, some 3-4000 years ago, but little is known of these sites, nor of how they functioned. They are often associated with burial remains, usually from cremations, though there is rarely any sign of a cairn or barrow and they are not interpreted as primarily burial sites. Fire is an important element and the activities at a Four Poster may well have included other ceremonial bonfires as well as those associated with death. They are also often associated with deposits of white quartz pebbles: quartz is a powerful stone whose potency continues to be recognized even in recent times.

The use of any Four Poster must have incorporated the landscape around it, but it can be hard for archaeologists to define and examine this without further upstanding remains. Certainly their landscape setting, on terraces at the side of the hillslopes overlooking the fertile valleys, is a common feature and must have been significant. Cultivation may well have extended further upslope in the Bronze Age to include the land where the Four Posters were built but they would still have been sited on the margins and they may well have helped to define the domestic farmed lands and hold them apart from the wilder moorlands.

Poltalloch: cup and ring marks
Argyll, NR 812 963
NR89NW 52

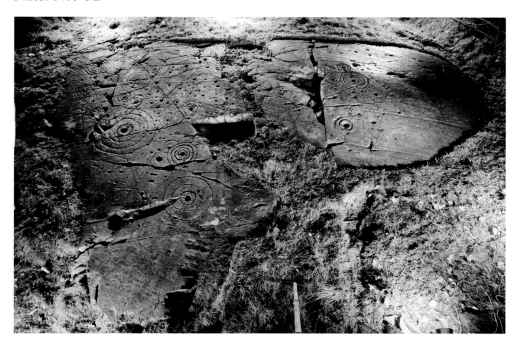

Cup and ring marks are common in Scotland, though their significance and meaning have long been lost. Some date back into the Neolithic, some 5000 years ago, but they were still current in the Bronze Age at least 1000 years later. Cup and ring marks occur in many different places. Some were made, as at Poltalloch, onto sheets of bedrock and these can be large impressive sites with complex arrangements of multiple rings, labyrinths, deep pitted cups and grooves. What can it all mean? Circular markings like this form a common theme that occurs in many places throughout the world, though it is unlikely that there were any connections: they are separated by wide gaps of time and space and make use of simple, recurrent symbols. Many possible interpretations have been put forward, from maps and markers in the landscape, to rites of passage and hallucinogenic journeys, or fertility symbols that echo the life-giving properties of water. All are equally likely, but without contact with their makers we can only surmise. What is clear, however, is that they were important and in some way tied up with ceremony and belief; many occur on standing stones and in stone settings, as at Ballymeanoch (see p176), and others were incorporated into burials. What then was the significance of those that appear to sit alone as at Poltalloch?

The work that went into making the cup and ring marks can only be imagined. Again this is an emphasis of their importance. They were made without the help of any metal tools, as the close up of the markings at Ormaig, Argyll (*NM 822 027, NM80SW 8*) shows. It is possible here to make out the individual peck marks of the stone tools that made them.

We can only speculate, however, on their original appearance: were they once coloured or given particular fillings? Ormaig is another site where considerable sheets of bedrock have been decorated, and the illustration from High Banks in Kircudbrightshire (*NX 709 489, NX74NW 43*) gives a good idea of the density of decoration that was sometimes achieved.

Many cup and ring mark sites lie on the upper slopes of hillsides. Because of this it has been suggested that view may well have been important, and indeed many do give spectacular vistas, often across important inland routeways or coastal landings. It also means, however, that many sit within, or at the edge of, modern forestry, particularly in the south-west of Scotland, and it is important to remember that forestry like this is an entirely modern construct and would not have been an element of the landscape familiar to their makers.

The detail from Garth Bothy (*Perthshire, NN 757 503, NN75SE 7*) shows how cup-marked stones may still be useful, though some locations can be deceptive. Here a small cup-marked stone has been incorporated into the gable wall of a modern cottage. Another cup-marked stone has been recorded in the vicinity, both once part of the prehistoric landscape of the area.

Inverurie: Pictish symbol stone
Aberdeenshire, NJ 780 206
NJ72SE 11

This stone is one of four from the churchyard at Inverurie. None is now in its original position, and we can only surmise where they once stood, but it is likely that they were associated with this location and they may have marked the site of graves. They are recorded as having been a part of the materials of the old church here, whence they were incorporated into the churchyard walls before being set up outside once more.

These stones all date to the Pictish period, some 1500 years ago. The Picts are well known for their lively art, which only survives in stone and on some metal jewellery, though it may well have found other forms of expression that have not withstood the test of time, such as work on leather or textiles. Pictish art follows clear patterns, which tend to be repeated, and which are not easy to interpret. This stone, however, depicts a spirited horse that one can well imagine to have been a particular, living, beast. Pictish art is remarkable for it is the first time that we get a glimpse of the local people of Scotland. While many images were abstract, others were drawn from life, and the incorporation of the human image onto their stones provides us with a uniquely personal link. Their style of clothing, and their pastimes, may have been different to those of today, but we can sense that they were subject to the same emotional triumphs and pressures.

The Picts did adopt Christianity, though is impossible to say whether this stone, if it did mark a burial, was Christian or not. Many Christian sites incorporated pagan contexts and it is perhaps not surprising that in the Pictish heartlands of Scotland many ancient church sites have Pictish remains. At St Finan's Church, Migvie (*Aberdeenshire, NJ 436 068, NJ40NW 2*) a Pictish Cross Slab stands by the entrance to the west side of the graveyard. This is a religious site of some antiquity — it is recorded as having been granted to the priory of St Andrew's in the twelfth century — but the stone must pre-date that by several centuries. The present church is relatively recent, but the site of an older building can just be made out as a low grass covered mound to the south.

The cross slab at Migvie is not as accomplished in its layout and execution as some Pictish monuments, but in some ways that adds to its attraction. The cross itself is filled by a complex of intertwined knots. Interestingly, two loops have been carved at the top of the cross, and it has been suggested that these are depictions of hanging loops. They may well represent the way in which a small metal cross could be suspended, but it has also been noted that loops such as this would commonly be used to suspend a tapestry. Tapestries would certainly have been a familiar sight in many Pictish households, and a design such as this could have been richly executed in cloth. If so, we can only imagine the colours that might have been employed. Sadly, cloth tends to decay much faster than other materials and there are no surviving examples of Pictish art made in this way, but this stone is an important reminder of the deficiencies of the archaeological record.

In the angles of the cross the sculptor carved some of the common Pictish symbols. To the upper left there is a double disc and z-rod; on the upper right a horseshoe with a v-rod; bottom left a pair of shears; and bottom right a man on horseback. The meaning of these symbols is not known, though they may have represented a specific family or allegiance. There is another mounted figure on the rear of the cross and it may have been made to commemorate a particular family, or death. Nineteenth-century records report that the cross was re-erected on this spot, having fallen and been found below ground level.

Campbeltown: St Ciaran's Cave
Argyll, NR 765 170
NR71NE 1

Caves have long held a fascination in Scotland. They tend to be visible in the landscape and they hold the potential of leading to diverse places, both real and imaginary. In addition, they can provide shelter and protection, as well as often offering a good view of the surrounding land or seascape. It is little surprise, therefore, that caves have been used in many ways since earliest times, both as homes and hideouts, as well as for more special, perhaps ceremonial, or religious reasons.

St Ciaran's Cave lies at the south end of the Kintyre peninsula. It is one of a group of caves that can be reached from the foreshore, but access may be difficult. As with all caves, its appearance is deceptive: despite the natural appearance of the exterior there is considerable evidence for human activity within the cave, and at one time the entrance itself was sealed off by a stone wall. This particular cave is traditionally associated with St Ciaran. Ciaran was an Irish monk of the early sixth century. He settled at Clonmacnois where he founded an abbey in 548. Ciaran was well travelled, and is recorded as an established local patron in the Campbeltown area — there was a church dedicated to him in Campbeltown from at least the mid-thirteenth century and the association may well have gone back earlier. Whether he actually visited the cave can never be known, but it is quite possible that those for whom it was a place of worship were well acquainted with Ciaran and his holy reputation.

The exterior wall to the cave is now much overgrown, but analysis has shown that it was set with lime mortar which means that it is unlikely to be older than the twelfth century. Inside the cave, however, the evidence suggests that there may have been earlier activity. The interior was examined by excavation in the 1920s, when traces of various internal structures were noted. These included a small building, a long stone-lined hollow, and a stone basin. In addition, there are several carvings, at least one of which has been paralleled with work dating to the Early Christian period (between the seventh and twelfth centuries AD), though many others are initials cut in more recent centuries. A sandstone slab on the floor may have formed the base for an upright stone, possibly a cross.

There is little to mark St Ciaran's Cave as special today, but it was clearly well used in the past and the signs suggest that that use may date to the Early Christian period.

Sgorr nam Ban-Naomha: cashel
Canna, NG 229 043
NG20SW 2

At the foot of some impressive cliffs on the south coast of Canna lie the ruins of a circular dry-stone enclosure containing the footings of several smaller structures. The name of this site translates as the Skerry of the Holy Women, and it seems to be a cashel or monastic settlement relating to the Celtic Church, dating to sometime around the seventh century AD.

The site would have been relatively isolated and hard of access, even in the past. It lies on a rocky terrace above the sea, at the foot of a stony scree below steep cliffs, and is only accessible from the sea in good weather. There are no written records that relate to the religious community here, but inaccessible spots like this are typical of those favoured at the time for a life of contemplation and devotion to God.

The remains of at least seven structures have been identified, but some are likely to relate to more recent activity, perhaps animal pens. Of those that seem to relate to the monastery one contains a well, from which water was directed in a carefully built stone channel through another building. It is an unusual arrangement and may have related to a bathhouse and the use of the water for particular curative powers. In this respect it is interesting to note that even in more recent times the local islanders regarded the conduit leading away from the well as of particular importance and they visited the site from time to time to check that it was not blocked.

Another structure within the compound contains a stone setting that is locally known as an 'altar', though there is no clear evidence for this, and the footings of a rectangular building set outside the entrance to the enclosure have been suggested as a possible church. Other buildings from this time would have related to individual cells for the inhabitants, but the remains have no doubt been blurred by their incorporation into more recent structures over the years.

There are other sites that indicate the considerable importance of the early Church on Canna. In common with the other western islands it was clearly fertile ground for the new religion and it is notable that Sgorr nam Ban-Naomha has generally been well known and venerated on the island over the centuries since it was abandoned.

See **colour plate 30**

Kame of Isbister: monastic settlement
Shetland, HU 391 915
HU39SE 4

The Kame of Isbister is an isolated rock stack connected to the mainland by a narrow ridge. Tradition maintains that there used to be a path along the ridge, but this has long since disappeared into the sea and the ridge is now virtually impassable. However, aerial photography reveals the remains of a group of at least 19 buildings arranged on the top of the stack in two ordered rows and isolated by an apparently defensive wall from the gentler cliffs to the eastern, seaward, side.

The site has obviously attracted attention over the years, and in the 1870s it was excavated by one C.G. Cockburn who dug trenches in two of the structures. He found little except for ash and fire-cracked stone. More recently the site has been identified as the remains of a monastic settlement dating to the early Church sometime in the eighth century.

Christianity was brought to Shetland and Orkney by Irish missionaries in the seventh century AD. The extent to which the new religion was adopted by the local population is unknown, but in the following years a number of small communities were set up by Celtic monks who sought relative isolation for their devotions. Sites such as this were ideal for these communities and many similar remains have been identified round the coasts of the Northern and Western Isles. In most cases a sturdy, outwardly defensive, wall was built, and this served as much to symbolize the exclusion of the outside, secular, world, as to enclose the religious community.

Port An Fhir-Bhréige: cairns
Iona, NM 262 218
NM22SE 31

Archaeology is full of mysteries; at best many of our interpretations of past monuments can only be inspired guesses based on the scanty evidence available, together with information deduced from our own way of life or that of other cultures. These cairns on the raised beach at the southern end of Iona are one such site.

Over 50 cairns have been recorded here, each built of pebbles apparently collected from the surface of the raised beach. Most are small and simple low mounds of less than 1m in height, but there are two larger cairns that are almost 2m high and these are surrounded by broad ditches.

A cairn field like this would commonly be interpreted as the result of clearance, where generations of past farmers have piled the stones removed from their fields in order to assist ploughing and cultivation. Here, however, this is unlikely to be the case because the cairns lie on a pebble surface that would not have supported agriculture. Another explanation might be that they represent prehistoric burials. This has not been tested by recent excavation, but there is no record of burial remains having been found here in previous times. If they are burial cairns it is an unusually large cairn cemetery, perhaps surprisingly so given the small size of the island where they are located.

Tradition, however, offers another explanation. The cairns lie adjacent to the bay where St Columba is said to have landed when he came to Iona from Ireland, and this has always been a popular spot for pilgrims. Travellers to Iona from the eighteenth century onwards have commented on the cairns, and the early journals record that they were said to have been built as acts of penance in earlier times by the monks who lived there and by pilgrims to the island. We shall never be certain of their origin, but the possibility that they may have been erected and added to as acts of devotion and penitence by those who came to visit the bays remains a strong one. Even today people frequently add a stone to the cairns to be found at the summit of many mountains or other landmarks, and this may be a tradition of some antiquity in Scotland.

Parc-an-Caipel, Congash: burial ground and Pictish symbol stones
Inverness-shire, NJ 058 262
NJ02NE 1

The photo shows clearly how agriculture can respect a known site. The patch of rough ground in the centre of this field marks the site of an old chapel and burial ground. This site has always been known locally, though there is no recorded documentation and therefore little information about it.

The interior of the enclosure is very stony, but with careful examination the visitor can still make out the foundations of the rectangular chapel building. The site is enclosed by the remains of a low stony bank which is roughly circular in plan, and this might suggest an early date. The entrance lies on the south side and interestingly it is flanked by two upright slabs each of which is decorated with Pictish symbols. Most Pictish symbols seem to have been carved according to a strict pattern book and those at Parc-an-Caipel are no exception. The east stone bears an 'elephant' symbol below a 'horseshoe'. The west stone has been carved with a 'double-disc-and-Z-rod' symbol below an unusual symbol that may be a helmet with an arrow running through it. The exact meanings of these Pictish symbols have never been determined so it is impossible to determine the original purpose of the stones at Parc-an-Caipel. Elsewhere, however, Pictish stones have been associated with burial remains. This would clearly be a possibility for the Parc-an-Caipel stones: the Picts certainly embraced Christianity and the stones themselves could have been moved from original locations within the body of the graveyard and placed to mark the entrance to the holy ground. If so, this would make Parc-an-Caipel a very early religious site. Interestingly, a recent visitor to the site has noticed a previously unrecorded tenth-century

grave stone in the burial ground. This dates to a more recent period than that of the Pictish Stones, but it is a good indication that here we have a site of some antiquity.

In some ways it is amazing that a site as denuded as this has survived the depredations of agriculture over the centuries. It has clearly always been avoided, however, and today it is a stony spot amidst the field as successive generations of farmers have used this spot to dump the stones that they turned up during cultivation. This field clearance may not be a mark of respect, but it has, ironically, helped to preserve the site by turning it into a clearance heap that, while not quite hiding the remains, has made them too stony to plough.

Orsay Island: chapel
Islay, NR 164 516
NR15SE 1

Even an unpretentious rural building can often hide an interesting past and all may not be what it seems. This ruined structure is all that remains of St Orain's chapel on Orsay Island, Islay. It is not known when the chapel was founded, but the indications are that this is a religious site of some antiquity. St Orain was an early saint, better known for his association with Iona. In its early days the chapel on Orsay Island was clearly a thriving foundation and at some time the building was altered to make it larger, by the addition of an extension to the east. The date of the abandonment of the chapel is not known either, but there was still a chaplain in residence in 1556.

There was a burial ground associated with the chapel and it contained at least one grave of some standing. This is the grave of Hugh MacKay which dates to the late medieval period. It is a small vault, open at the west end, and built of roughly dressed stone, with a slab roof. In 1959 three fragments of a stone cross were found in the vicinity of Hugh MacKay's tomb. These date to the sixth to eighth centuries and they add substance to the argument for an early date for the foundation. Two of the fragments can be seen in the Islay Museum, though the third is now lost. There are said to have been other gravestones of interest here, but these were removed when the nearby lighthouse was built in the 1820s. It is also recorded that the eastern entrance to the consecrated ground was marked by a simple stone cross which now stands outside the south wall.

The burial ground was cleared and used as a garden by the lighthouse keepers throughout the nineteenth century. Apparently, however, it did not prove to be a fertile spot. It is recorded that nothing would grow there and it now comprises nothing more than a bare enclosure.

Kilmory Oib: cross slab and well
Argyll, NR 780 902
NR79SE 7

Over the last 1300 years Christianity has dominated in Scotland, and in veneration to it there are many small Christian monuments, predominately cross slabs, across the countryside. Here at Kilmory Oib a simple cross carved onto a rectangular slab has been set upright at one end of a stone tank from which flows a stream of water. The site is situated amongst ruined houses in land now used for commercial forestry.

In common with previous religions, Early Christianity recognized the particular life-giving power of water, as well as its slightly unpredictable state. Water could be hard to control and supplies might come and go, seemingly at their own authority. Water appeared to have a life of its own, and this could be celebrated, and perhaps directed, by the erection of a cross slab.

Other crosses were associated with structures. At Barnakill in Argyll (*NR 819 914, NR89SW 16 & 38*) a small ruinous building has been identified as an Early Christian Cell. Beside the nearby stream there is a rock which has been incised with a small cross, possibly a sanctuary marker for the site. Individual cells like this were an important feature of the early church, much used for quiet prayer and contemplation. The cell at Barnakill contains an aumbry, a small cupboard in the thickness of the wall, to house religious objects. This area of Argyll housed many flourishing religious communities in the early days of the Church and so the location of isolated cells here is not unexpected. The use of solitude to concentrate the mind and assist communion with God was well known from early times.

Some crosses may once have stood in more solitary positions. An impressive stone with its simple Celtic Cross stands just outside the graveyard at Creich in Sutherland (*NH 636 891, NH68NW 4*) where it is suggested that it may have marked a preaching spot in use prior to the construction of the medieval church. The stone itself is over 2m high, but the cross is a simple one. It is known as St Demhan's Cross after St Devenic, a Celtic saint. There has been a church at Creich at least since the thirteenth century and St Devenic was an early patron. A local fair dedicated to him is recorded as having taken place here, well into the seventeenth century. In the 1770s a new church was built in Creich, but it lies in ruins today.

See **colour plate 31**

Taynuilt: Nelson Monument
Argyll, NN 005 310
NN03SW 12

This impressive standing stone is, at least in its present role, a recent creation. It was erected in 1805, by workmen from the local furnace, on the top of a prominent rise to be a memorial to Lord Nelson who had recently died at the Battle of Trafalgar. The inscription on the north face provides the details and, as such, it is an important record for future archaeologists.

It is possible, however, that the stone has a genuine archaeological past as an antiquity. It was taken from a low ridge, some 2km away, where it was lying flat. Local tradition says, however, that there were other 'pillar' stones lying in the same field though there is no information as to their fate. It is therefore possible that there was once a stone circle or setting here, but it would be impossible to prove this without excavation to reveal the original stone holes and any other features. Certainly the stone is an impressive one, and prehistoric settings of similar stones are common in the vicinity, especially a few kilometres to the south around Kilmartin Glen.

Whatever the origins of the stone, the Nelson Monument at Taynuilt is a good example of how the practice of erecting standing stones has never quite gone out of fashion. It is also a good example of how we are constantly altering the landscape so that everything that we do today creates the archaeology of the future.

8 BURIALS IN THE LANDSCAPE

The disposal of the dead is intimately connected with people's religious beliefs. For the first few thousand years of prehistory it took place in such a way that did not leave any archaeological evidence. Or not any evidence that has, as yet, been recognized. But a shift in burial practice was one of the great suite of changes that took place with the adoption of farming some 5000 years ago. From then on the landscape of Scotland has been littered with the remains of her dead.

The early farming villages felt the need to mark their claim to the lands on which they lived. They also wished to commemorate the community of their ancestors and the two became closely intertwined. They built great palaces for the dead which were designed to be used over a long period of time (Kilchoan and Auchenlaich). These tombs included facilities for the participation of the living. Tombs like this also acted as prominent markers in the landscape and they served to reinforce the position of the local inhabitants within their territories.

With time the traditionally communal importance of the dead waned, mirroring the change reflected in the ceremonial sites. By the time cists like Sunday's Wells were used in the Bronze Age some 4000 years ago, the emphasis had changed to a celebration of the value of the individual. It was no longer necessary to re-enter a tomb, and this meant dramatic changes to the architecture associated with burial. Many sites were no longer so prominent in the landscape, though they may well have continued to serve as an anchor for the community. The ties between the people and their position in the land were still close though, and in some cases (Rashieburn), groups of monuments were still designed to provide an obvious marker.

Not surprisingly, given an increasing population, considerable cultural diversity began to develop both within and between societies, so that there are many different expressions of burial practice from now on. Some of this is shown here with the inclusion of sites like Ninewells and Rullion Green. Though much of the population seem to have been given more simple burials that have not survived, this diversity continued into the Iron Age as may be seen by the introduction of various types of square burials (Lettie's Grave and Red Castle).

With the coming of Christianity more uniform practices were once again established across the country, though there was still scope for considerable variation in individual detail. Fintray, Boulterhall, Conagearaidh and New Ulva all show how the application of one basic set of beliefs and practices can lead to a wealth of different information in the surviving monuments.

Today, of course, we have our own practices and these vary considerably across society. It is interesting to note that with the rise in cremation we have returned to the situation

of 8000 years ago when the disposal of most of our dead leaves little archaeological trace. How would the archaeologist of tomorrow interpret the ceremonial, but often industrial-scale, buildings of the modern crematorium?

Kilchoan: chambered tomb
Argyll, NR 807 964
NR89NW 12

Chambered tombs like that seen in **colour plate 32** are a common feature of the Scottish landscape. They mark the spot where the early farming population chose to bury their dead, some 5000 years ago. A sense of place was important at this time and these great houses of stone were built to serve as a link between the living community, their dead ancestors and the land itself. We do not know whether everyone was buried in this way, but the chambered tombs housed many of the population. They were designed to be used over and over again, so that they could be re-entered with new bodies as people died. In general these tombs comprised a central chamber, which might be subdivided — this was reached via a low passage through a mound of cairn material which covered the central stone work and was often sealed by turf. The outside appearance of the tombs varied greatly from area to area: some had surrounding kerbs, often with fancy stone work; some had elaborate forecourts; some were round, others long or trapezoidal; most had some form of blocking to the main entrance that could be moved aside to admit entry when necessary.

There is evidence around Scotland for considerable variation in the precise burial rites that were used, but the one common feature is that the dead were not buried and forgotten. The tombs were designed to allow continued contact between the living and the dead. In some cases bodies were exposed prior to placement inside a tomb, in other cases they were inserted directly; in some cases the bones were kept together, in other cases they were disarticulated so that skulls, for example, could be placed separately to long bones. Occasionally cremation was used, and this became more popular with time. Sometimes there were elaborate grave goods, and sometimes there is evidence for accompanying animals which may have had a totemic function to reinforce the group identity of the community. Whatever the rite, a chambered tomb was a visible physical marker which emphasized the ancestry of a particular community within a particular territory. Some tombs were built in places where they commanded clear views across the landscape and could themselves be clearly seen from afar. Others were more discrete.

Like many religious centres today the tombs provided a focus to which the living could go. They were used in many ways: not only for the immediate ceremonies after a death, but also as a place to keep in touch with your ancestral family. There is increasing evidence that they were designed to assist communication with the wider spiritual world. Several tombs have communications systems that appear to lead nowhere; some have minute chambers that connect into the tomb; others have carefully placed stones that allow noise, or light, to pass into or out of the central chamber. The siting of the tombs was clearly of vital importance: light from the sun at a particular time of the year; moonlight; views to specific stars — all came into play and provide hints as to the spiritual connections that were important at the time.

These tombs were once grand, turf-covered monuments, but time has taken its toll and at many sites only the central chamber survives. At Kilchoan there is a hint of a low stony mound around the chamber to suggest the original dimensions of the site. Many

of the cairn stones were robbed to build local stone dykes in recent times. The tomb was excavated in 1864, when evidence for cremated bones was found together with objects including broken fragments of pottery, and flaked stone tools such as flint scrapers and flakes. The chamber itself is divided into three compartments, and is built of massive blocks which stand as testimony to the skills of the local community. Similar skills are seen at Achaidh in Sutherland (*NH 671 911, NH69SE 7*), where the chamber of a tomb has survived stone robbing that has denuded much of the surrounding cairn. This tomb was excavated at the start of the twentieth century and found to contain an unburnt skeleton.

See **colour plate 32**

Auchenlaich: long cairn
Perthshire, NN 649 071
NN60NW 4

It is often more difficult to recognize the traces of past populations in the fertile lands where millennia of agriculture have taken their toll. In addition, different local conditions may mean that monuments were constructed out of materials that have not been so suited to withstand the test of time. New monuments are still to be found every year. The farmed landscape in this picture has served to blur the archaeological remains that lie within it, but the remarkable long cairn of Auchenlaich is now under statutory protection and its remains may just be made out. This denuded cairn was first seriously examined in the late 1980s. It is visible as a rickle of rough ground that connects the two trees in the centre of the photograph. This rough ground comprises a mound, now no more than 0.5m high, with the remains of a chamber at one end (the south-east) and a possible second chamber roughly halfway along its length. There is evidence at the south-east end that there was originally a concave forecourt from which the chamber could be accessed.

Auchenlaich was clearly an important monument — a tomb built for the local farming community some 5000 years ago. They designed the forecourt to provide space for gatherings and ceremonies, and came here to honour their ancestors and reinforce their spiritual links with the land. In time the monument fell out of use and the importance of the ancestral community was forgotten. Farming took over and gradually encroached upon the site; evidence of medieval cultivation was found when the monument was examined in 1995 (Strachan 1995).

The landscape is not static and change continues today. The farmed landscape of this picture is now very different as agriculture has given way to new economies. At

213

Auchenlaich a caravan site and extraction works dominate the landscape of today. Change has always taken place, however, and it would be foolish to fossilize the landscape as we know it. Nevertheless, the traces of the past that survive today help us to build an understanding of the landscape as we see it. It is important to record them and it is vital that enough monuments should be protected to aid that understanding.

Landscape change and damage to monuments is not just a thing of the fertile south, however. At Allt Sgiathaig in Assynt (*NC 234 255, NC22NW 1*) a low mound of cairn material denotes the position of a much denuded tomb. The chamber is ruinous and only a few of its original side slabs still stand. This tomb has been much damaged both in the past and in more recent times when improvements to the nearby road caused the ground to be cut away at the edge of the cairn. The barren countryside of today gives little impression of the Neolithic 5000 years ago: patchy woodland would have been more common, and the presence of the tomb indicates a higher degree of fertility for the land than we might guess at. There was clearly a local farming community to whom this area was important enough for it to be used as the link with their ancestors.

Sunday's Wells: cist burial
Aberdeenshire, NJ 617 039
NJ60SW 3

Abundant evidence for prehistoric burial was found at Sunday's Wells in the late nineteenth century. This evidence was said to comprise numerous cairns together with small, box-like, stone cists.

The use of cists for individual burial marks a change that took place some 4000 years ago when new customs were developing along with the introduction of bronze. This is very different from the preceding Neolithic period, when communal, monumental, tombs were preferred. There was a marked rise in the importance of the individual in the Bronze Age which came about for many reasons. At first, metal goods were neither abundant nor common and it would be many millennia before they became an essential part of life for everyone. The first metal goods were made of copper, bronze and gold, and they are likely to have been the treasured possessions of a favoured few — the elite. The possession of metal was something that could single out the individual and it is likely that society became increasingly stratified, but there was another facet to this. For the first time there was an 'everyday' artefact for which the raw materials were relatively rare and which had to be specially worked. Metal goods could not be made by just anyone, and the evidence suggests that there were travelling metal-smiths who made and traded goods as they moved around.

Burial can be a remarkably transparent window onto society, and Bronze Age cists demonstrate that some (probably not all) members of society were laid to rest in individual stone boxes and provided with grave goods, including food and drink, with which to face

the afterlife. Many of the grave goods have long since disappeared into Scotland's acid soils, but surviving objects include pottery vessels together with stone arrowheads and other archery equipment; jewellery was also common. Not surprisingly, metal goods such as daggers were sometimes added, no doubt to emphasize the importance of the deceased.

The occupants of the cists were inhumed with their bodies drawn up into a foetal position, and presumably bound in some sort of shroud. Few human remains have

survived, but on occasion, as at West Puldrite in Orkney (*HY414 185, HY41NW 1*), skeletons are found. The cist at West Puldrite lay below a mound which was excavated in the 1920s. Unusually, it contained three skeletons with no grave goods. It was impossible to say whether the first two skeletons had been buried together, but both bodies had been pushed aside to make way for the third burial.

Although some cists are associated with mounds, so that the grave sites are quite visible in the landscape, many are not. Most have no noticeable marker, or none that has survived today, and it is still not uncommon for cists to be uncovered during development work. This is nicely illustrated by the photograph from Stevenston, Ayrshire (*NS 266 420, NS24SE 16*) where a cist was found just below the ground surface during the digging of foundations at the end of the nineteenth century. There was no skeleton, but the cist contained a particular type of pot, known as a food vessel, together with a stone 'club'.

Ninewells: cairn
Perthshire, NO 075 436
NO04SE 1

Although it is true that the landscape of Scotland was covered by a greater density of trees in the past, forestry plantations such as this give little idea of the early woodland. It is likely that this monument originally sat in more open ground. The trees in the picture are recent.

This site is a cairn — a mound of stones that was raised in the Bronze Age, nearly 4000 years ago — to cover a series of individual burials. It has, however, undergone some depredation with time: in 1865 it was noted that the stones were removed from time to time for 'modern use'. Because of this it is impossible to know the original configuration of the cairn and the burials it once contained, but some information can be gleaned from the remains.

The mound itself sat on a stony platform which may well have been deliberately made. A series of stones surrounded the cairn to form a kerb, and 25 of these stones survive. Originally it can be estimated that there must have been about 30 stones and they were carefully set into position with the largest to the south-west and the others graded in size away from this. One of the surviving stones was decorated in the Bronze Age with four pecked cup-markings. Little remains of the stony mound inside the kerb, so the precise nature of the burials remains a mystery, but the cairn is likely to have been built over at least one burial, which may or may not have been in a cist, and other individual burials may well have been inserted into the sides after it was erected. There has been no modern excavation of this site, but there is evidence of some uncontrolled digging. Unfortunately

218

monuments such as this are still vulnerable to those who feel that they should contain buried treasure. Sadly for them, and the site, little of value is ever found, and the lasting damage done to the remains can obscure important archaeological information that helps build up a picture of life in the past. In this case it is recorded that broken chunks and chips of white quartz were up-cast after the digging of a hole in the centre. Quartz is a powerful stone that has long held an important place in mythology and it is frequently found in association with burial sites both from the Bronze Age and more recent times.

Ninewells would have been an impressive monument in the fertile Bronze Age landscape of south-east Perthshire.

Glennan: cairns
Argyll, NM 856 011
NM80SE 30

Cairns were frequently raised in groups, but they are often so denuded today that little remains. Here, to the south-west of Creaganterve Beg farm, lie a couple of cairns that now blend well into the cultivated background. They may be seen in the stony ground to the front of the tree. The larger cairn stands just over 1m high, and it has been disturbed in the centre to reveal an up-turned slab that once covered a cist. There is no sign of the original cist burial, but the covering stone was decorated in prehistory by the pecking of at least nine cup-marks. The meaning of carvings like this has been long forgotten, but they are a common feature of Bronze Age sites and frequently occur on both exposed outcrops of bedrock and on slabs, such as this, used in cist burials and sometimes as standing stones.

The other cairn is smaller and lower. It too is disturbed at the centre where a clear hollow provides evidence of past 'diggings'. Uncontrolled digging like this rarely provided any hoped-for treasure, but it makes a double loss because it was rarely well recorded and so it has also deprived us of valuable information relating to these early inhabitants of Scotland.

By the late nineteenth century, as people became more aware of the importance of digging carefully to investigate and record the contents of archaeological sites *in situ*, those who were keen to investigate them did sometimes keep records. These can often be of great value today as they help to add detail to the archaeological record and they give a good idea of the size of many monuments before intensive agriculture and other

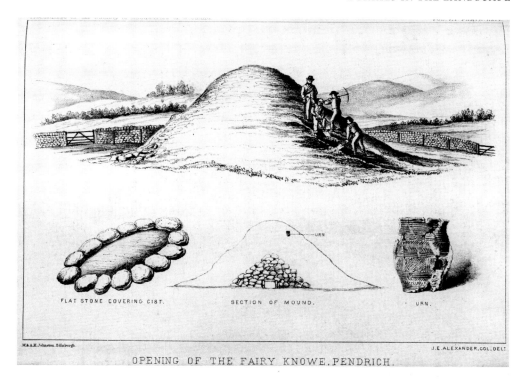

FLAT STONE COVERING CIST.   SECTION OF MOUND.   URN.

OPENING OF THE FAIRY KNOWE, PENDRICH.

modern developments took their toll. In 1868 one such excavator was J.E. Alexander of Stirling who used workmen to drive a trench through a local cairn known as the Fairy Knowe (*Stirling, NS 796 981, NS79NE 1*). He was careful to keep notes on the work, and these were published in the *Proceedings of the Society of Antiquaries of Scotland* in 1870. They included some fine drawings, both of the state of the cairn prior to excavation, and of the findings.

At the centre of the cairn Alexander found a stone cist which lay on the old ground surface and contained charcoal together with fragments of human bone. Although the cist was covered by a stone pile, the body of the mound was composed of earth within which he found more charcoal, blackened stones, and fragments of human and animal bone. There were no obvious grave goods in the cist, but some material was found in the mound, including six flint arrowheads and fragments of at least two pots, one of which was a Beaker, from the early Bronze Age.

Fairy Knowe may still be seen, though it is greatly reduced in size: before excavation it is said to have been some 25m in diameter and over 6m high, but today it is 18m across and only 2.2m high.

221

The Five Hillocks, Rashieburn: barrows
Orkney, Holm, HY 459 053
HY40NE 4

The mounds on the horizon comprise a series of earthen barrows which were raised in the Bronze Age, up to 4000 years ago. Each was built to cover one or more burials, and it is likely that a barrow cemetery such as this contained the dead from one community.

Despite the name of this group there are actually eight barrows on the hillside here, with a low bank which runs around them. Each mound has a shallow depression in the top: an indication of someone's quest for 'treasure' in times past, though it is unlikely that anything of monetary value was found. There is little indication of the exact way in which the individual burials were inserted into the mounds. However, it is likely that some of the graves comprised stone cists, and a possible indication of this may be seen in one barrow where the central diggings have extended down far enough to reveal a single stone that may once have formed part of a cist. Other burials may have been made directly into the earthen mound material, and it is possible that both inhumation and cremation were involved. The dead in the Bronze Age were frequently given some grave goods such as a pot containing food or drink and the tools of their trade or weapons, but there has been no sign of this at Rashieburn, though prehistoric objects have occasionally been turned up in the surrounding fields by the local farmer. Orkney is a fertile place, and it is likely that the population in the Bronze Age may have numbered as many people as today.

Barrows such as these were a common feature of the Bronze Age where burial rites had shifted to an emphasis on the individual, rather than the great communal tombs of the Neolithic. They were clearly designed to be used in a different way to the long-lived

222

Neolithic tombs. Repeated access for active contact with the spirits of the dead was no longer important, though mounds like these would ensure that the dead were not forgotten. The mounds continued to serve as an important link between the living community, their dead ancestors and their land. Some barrows occur alone, others in groups or cemeteries. The surrounding bank at Rashieburn is not common, but others may have been lost to ploughing in the past, and it presumably helped to demarcate the sacred area. In other areas mounds of stone were raised to cover the dead, and these are known as cairns. Another name once commonly used and still appearing on many maps is tumuli.

Barrows or cairns such as these were designed to be markers in the landscape as much as to house, and honour, the dead. As the photograph shows they can be very prominent, though they rarely attain the size and complexity of the great chambered tombs of the Neolithic. Like the mounds at Rashieburn, barrow cemeteries were often carefully sited to take advantages of false crests so that they were clearly visible to those who worked the land below.

Rullion Green: ring enclosures
Midlothian, NT 220 622
NT26SW 8

Some burial remains are hard to see on the ground and these may be best viewed from the air. The Bronze Age cemetery at Rullion Green, just outside Edinburgh (about 2500 years old) is one of these. Though the slight circular banks, known as ring enclosures, are visible as you walk across the field it is only from a height that the pattern of the remains can be made out. At Broughton Knowe, Peeblesshire (*NT 098 388, NT03NE 17*) it has been possible to photograph a ring enclosure in the lengthening evening sunlight, but it is still aerial photography, such as that for Rullion Green, which gives the best impression of a whole cemetery.

The remains at Rullion Green today are covered by grass. They survive as low circular banks with an outer ditch and a level platform area in the centre. A total of 11 rings have

been recorded here and there has been some excavation on two separate occasions. In 1948 the excavation of one of the larger enclosures revealed a circular burial area that had been covered by a wooden wigwam type of structure. This was set into the ditch and leant against the internal bank for support. A single post had stood at the centre of the structure and to one side of this lay the remains of a cremation. There were no obvious grave goods, but a handful of flint flakes were recovered.

A further eight of the enclosures were excavated between 1983-5. These provided a date for the burials of 635+/-105 BC (GU-1755) and they confirmed that each enclosure contained cremated remains which lay on a prepared surface at the centre. One again there were no obvious grave goods, but a general scatter of stone tools provided additional evidence relating to the material culture of those who used this site.

Rullion Green today lies at the edge of the cultivated land. This area may not have been much different in the Bronze Age, though the woodland would not have been confined to the regulated patterns of the modern forestry plantations. While the precise details of local land use may have varied, Bronze Age cultivation is likely to have respected the site itself; the Bronze Age farmers whose settlements were scattered through the Pentlands would still recognize much of the area today.

Strontollier: kerb cairn
Argyll, NM 907 289
NM92NW 7

Although many burial mounds in prehistory were designed to be large upstanding monuments, this was not always the case. It is doubtful whether kerb cairns such as this, just to the north side of the road through Glen Lonan in Argyll, ever stood much than 1m in height.

Kerb cairns comprise low circular mounds with a kerb of large stones or boulders. As here, they are frequently associated with other monuments such as standing stones and stone circles, and they are generally thought to have been in use in the period between 2000-1000 BC, in the Bronze Age. Where they have been excavated there is evidence that they were initially used to house one burial only, sometimes inhumation and sometimes cremation.

The small kerb cairn at Strontollier was excavated by the RCAHMS in 1967. Originally, it had a kerb of 15 large boulders, but only 12 survive today. These had been carefully set with the largest to the south of the cairn and they gradually decreased to the north. At the base of the kerbstones there was evidence for a layer of white quartz chips. This site was associated with a cremation burial: there was a clear layer of burning on the old land surface, together with a shallow hollow, and a small amount of cremated bone had been incorporated into the base of the mound above.

Just to the west of the cairn stands a lone standing stone and there is a stone circle close by. Another group of cairns lies to the south-west, some 3.5km away at the other end of Loch Nell. This was clearly an important area in the Bronze Age, but it is interesting to note that tradition would associate it with more recent times: the standing stone is known locally as Clach Dhiarmaid (in various forms), and together with the cairn it is said to mark the spot where Diarmaid, an Irish hero, died and was buried.

Lettie's Grave: square cairn
Sutherland, NC 692 052
NC60NE 1

Here, the scanty remains of stone structures above the Lettie river in Sutherland mark a site locally known as the burial place of a chieftain. This cannot be substantiated without excavation (and even then it might be difficult), but it is worth remembering that oral traditions such as this have sometimes been shown to be surprisingly accurate. The structures themselves seem to be associated with burial, and they would generally be dated to the immediate period after the Roman occupation of Scotland in the early centuries AD. Unlike earlier burial remains these tombs are square.

There are three rectangular structures here. Each comprises a stone cairn inside a square kerb built of horizontal slabs, with larger posts at the corners. Each is ruinous.

The abundance of stone in Sutherland has assisted the survival of this site, but the lack of information from modern excavation, or even from antiquarian journals, means that the mystery of Lettie's Grave remains.

Elsewhere in Scotland other square burials exist. Many were constructed of earth, with little or no stone. This is a burial type that was current from the pre-Roman period into later Pictish times and not surprisingly a great variety of rituals at death is reflected in the remains. Some comprise cist graves; others are simple pits. Some people were buried alone; others were buried in cemeteries. Some were buried in caves, some in houses, and in some cases burials were set into pre-existing monuments.

Earthen barrows have often suffered greatly from the depredations of the plough. Most are visible only as crop marks which capture particular conditions within a cultivated field. At Pitgaveny House, Morayshire (*NJ 243 655, NJ26NW 37*), a cemetery of several square barrows may be seen clearly on the aerial photograph, cut

by the modern tracks of the tractor. Barrow cemeteries similar to this occur throughout Europe and many have been excavated, as at Red Castle in Angus (*NO 687 508, NO65SE 18*). These were clearly the burial places of people of some social standing and importance. They were usually given their own individual barrow, and buried in a central pit, sometimes with possessions.

The Cat Stane: inscribed standing stone and burials
Midlothian, NT 148 743
NT17SW 1

This site is remarkable for its current location: just to the north of one of the runways for Edinburgh Airport. It is a good example of how the current landscape does not always reflect that of the past. This is an interesting site that has clearly been important since the standing stone was first erected sometime in the Bronze Age, 3-4000 years ago. At that time the stone that we now know as the Cat Stane seems to have formed part of the kerb to a large cairn, some 6m in diameter. This was described by a visitor in 1699 as a low cairn with big horizontal kerbstones. Some 50m to the west there stood a large barrow, now completely obliterated, but when it was excavated in 1824 it was found to contain several skeletons. This patch of land was clearly of considerable religious significance.

The cairn at the Cat Stane itself was also excavated in the 1860s, but no human remains were found, though there is some indication that it may have covered a rough stone cist. All traces of the other kerb stones have long gone; they were much smaller than the Cat Stane which apparently towered above them like a marker. In the late fifth or early sixth century AD an inscription was carved onto the eastern face. The words are no longer clear, but it has been translated as, 'In this tomb lies Vetta, daughter of Victricius'. Vetta and her father were presumably people of some standing — members of the Votadini, the local tribe at the time. It is impossible to say whether she was actually buried below the stone,

but to one side a large Early Christian cemetery has been found that dates to these times. The cemetery has been excavated on several occasions, in the nineteenth century and in more recent times, though it has never been completely examined. It comprised over 50 long stone cists carefully laid out in rows. The individual graves were oriented east-west with the head to the west, and many still contained fragmentary skeletal remains. There were no grave goods, but there were signs that the cemetery had once been enclosed within a stone wall.

Few sites like this have survived in the fertile lowlands of the Lothians. The Cat Stane is a good reminder of the density of past populations who, like us, apparently took an interest in monuments from earlier times. We can never know exactly what they made of them, but the Cat Stane is not alone as an example of a site that has been reused.

Fintray, St Meddan's Church: flat tombstone
Aberdeenshire, NJ 871 155
NJ81NE 11

There has been a church on this spot since medieval times, when the land belonged to the Abbey of Lindores in Fife. The present building went out of use in 1703, when it was replaced by a new church at Hatton of Fintray, which was itself replaced by the present parish church.

The graveyard at St Meddan's is clearly of some antiquity, and there are several early gravestones, as well as fragments of small sculptured stones which show that over the ages the local population has included people of substance. In addition to the two crosses on this grave slab some information about the interment below may be deduced from the sword. This is, presumably, a man's grave, and in keeping with his times he was clearly a warrior.

233

Boulterhall: tomb
Fife, NO 416 244
NO42SW 1

Even recent burials have often suffered the depredations of time. Though there was a fashion in recent centuries for ornate tombs, they have not all stood up well to the elements, and not all were collected together in graveyards. The countryside still contains the remains of many individual burials where the decision was made, usually because of particular personal attachments, to lay someone to rest away from the usual locations.

This small tomb was originally enclosed by a stone dike which has been removed. The tomb itself comprises a barrel-vaulted structure which was set into the ground. The entrance, at the north, is the only end visible today. Above the entrance there was originally a carved stone pediment with the date of 1647 and a shield flanked by the initials A and N. This is now very eroded by weathering, but it was intended to provide identification for Alexander Nairne of nearby Sandfuird. Nairne was killed in London in 1642. He died in a street riot, but it was clearly important that he be finally laid to rest among the peaceful Fife countryside. As in earlier times, his tomb was designed to ensure that he should not be forgotten and to reinforce his links with the land that had been important to him and his family.

Conagearaidh: old burial ground and settlement
Canna, Small Isles, NG 216 057
NG20NW 18

The remains of the small settlement of Conagearaidh lie on the north shores of the western end of Canna, below a series of imposing cliffs, well away from the main habitations on the island today (**colour plate 33**). The settlement was never large: the remains indicate five buildings at the most, not all of which were necessarily houses and two of which overlie others. In common with many other small settlements across the Highlands and Islands it was a self contained place, and provision was made for the dead to be buried locally in a small graveyard which was kept apart from agriculture and livestock by the erection of a stone dike. Graveyards such as this soon revert to nature once the dikes are no longer maintained and plants and animals are able once again to encroach within, but a careful eye can still spot many of the remains.

In 1805 this spot is depicted on an estate map of Canna, and the settlement was obviously in use at the time. By 1881, however, it appears to have been ruinous when visited by the map-makers of the Ordnance Survey. As well as the buildings there are a number of enclosures and one of these, to the right of the photograph, just above a modern stone enclosure, can be seen to contain upright stone markers. This is the burial ground: it contains at least five burial-plots marked out by settings of smaller stones taken from the beach, and there are also two clear grave slabs. The names of those who lie in rest here have long gone, but this small cemetery was clearly an important spot for the local community. Like the burial mounds of long ago, it served to emphasize the links between the community and their land and to ensure that the dead were not forgotten.

Interestingly, there is also another burial at Conagearaidh. It lies to the west of the graveyard, across the burn and on the other side of the houses, and it is marked by a wooden cross set into a base of stones at one end of a long shallow depression. The reasons why this grave was set apart have long been forgotten.

A close-up of the burial ground at New Ulva in Argyll (*NR 705 802, NR78SW 11*) gives an idea of the condition of many of these graveyards once they are no longer maintained. Here, too, there was a stone dike to enclose the graves which were set in an area that had been levelled into the hillslope. It has been suggested that this graveyard may be of Early Christian date, due to the presence of a larger rectangular grave setting with a marker stone at each corner. It is impossible to confirm the date without excavation, however, and it is likely that it went on in use into much more recent times.

Close to the burial ground at New Ulva lies another ruinous enclosure which is locally reputed to have been used for the burial of unbaptised infants. This would be hard to substantiate, but cemeteries such as this were an important feature of many communities from the medieval period on. They were commonly used not only for infant burials, but also for others such as the unknown victims of shipwrecks who might wash up locally, as well as victims of murder and certain diseases. It was not unusual in these cases for the graves to be unmarked, a fact which does not help the archaeologist seeking to record and understand them.

See **colour plate 33**

9 THE WORK OF THE NATIONAL MONUMENTS RECORD FOR SCOTLAND

The illustrations in the book are drawn from the archives of the National Monuments Record for Scotland (NMRS) which is part of the Royal Commission on the Ancient and Historical Monuments for Scotland (RCAHMS; http://www.rcahms.gov.uk) housed in a purpose-built building in Bernard Terrace on the south side of Edinburgh. The NMRS curates and provides public access to the material records (mainly photographs and papers) relating to the known archaeological sites and historic buildings and monuments of Scotland. This is not a simple task, however, and to fully understand the work of the NMRS it is necessary first to understand something of the work of the RCAHMS.

The Royal Commission on the Ancient and Historical Monuments for Scotland was established by Royal Warrant in 1908. It was set up to make a list of all known archaeological monuments in Scotland from the earliest times up to 1707. It is unusual for a Royal Commission to still be in existence after so many years, as most Royal Commissions are convened to look into a particular problem, make a report, and then close down. It is a sign of the enormity of the task assigned to RCAHMS, and of its changing role and accumulation of additional responsibilities, that has led to its continued existence. RCAHMS is now regarded as an important element of the Scottish archaeological scene.

In the beginning, RCAHMS tackled its task by working through the archaeological monuments on a county by county basis. There was one employee, the Secretary to the Commissioners, A.O. Curle, and he set out on his bicycle to visit every archaeological site in a county and make a record of its known history and present state. The first county recorded was Berwickshire, and it took 18 months to complete. Very quickly, however, it was realised that the task was not as simple as it had seemed. New sites were still being discovered and, not surprisingly, the staff of the RCAHMS found that when they actually went out to look for sites the numbers of monuments known in any one area went up dramatically.

The work of the RCAHMS is particularly important because it does not only deal with sites that are large or obvious, nor only with sites that are in a particularly good state of repair. Under the RCAHMS scheme all traces of the past are afforded attention. This has resulted in the discovery and recording of many new sites and several new types of sites. The nature of archaeology is such that even now it is possible to recognize as archaeological remains features that would not have been paid any attention 20 years ago. This is particularly the case with the development of new techniques of field survey. RCAHMS today has a dedicated team of field surveyors who are able to apply their expertise to sophisticated electronic equipment which allows them not only to record the face of the countryside in great detail, but also, in certain instances, to look for traces of walls or ditches buried underneath it (Bowden 1999). The number of sites that they find is such that the original aim of producing a county-by-county register of ancient sites in Scotland has long since been abandoned. Survey work is now carried out on the basis of smaller geographical areas, chosen for a variety of reasons such as their vulnerability to development, or a lack of previous work in an area that comes to attention, for example in a land sale. In some cases the surveyors return to areas previously surveyed by RCAHMS in the early years of the twentieth century. New sites are inevitably found.

The number of sites recorded has also increased because the original cut-off point of 1707 has long since been abandoned. RCAHMS surveyors today can take into account much more recent features such as the archaeological remains that pertain to the two World Wars of the early twentieth century. Although early sites are still under threat and many are destroyed every year, new sites are also being created as the present generations make their mark on the land. The net result is an ever-increasing archaeological resource that needs careful recording and management if we are to know and understand fully our past history. One has only to look at the reaction of modern teenagers to the slag heaps and pit heads that were once such a familiar part of everyday life to see this process in action.

The work of the RCAHMS surveyors may be divided into three sections: landscape survey, detailed survey and aerial survey. Landscape survey comprises the recording of sites in their general setting and recognizes that archaeological sites do not exist in isolation. We cannot be sure of boundaries that were given to any particular geographical setting, nor of all the ways in which people chose to alter or manage the landscape, but by recording a site together with its neighbours and including the details of the landscape setting it is possible to get some hints of the past as a dynamic entity. In the same way it is important to record sites of different periods that occur in one place. Over time people were attracted to a place for different reasons and the shifting patterns of buildings and land use can give a clear picture of this.

Detailed survey comprises the closer-in picture of any one site. Many sites are very complex and underwent considerable change over time. For detailed survey a minute record of a single site is completed by the surveyors, which includes measured drawings, photographs and written descriptions. In this way information is collected which can enable archaeologists to study the developments and modifications that took place over the lifetime of the site. Though the popular image of archaeology is that of the intrepid excavator, excavation is a destructive tool that archaeologists only use *in extremis*. Survey work such as that of the RCAHMS can provide a wealth of detail that helps us to better understand our past, while preserving the integrity of the sites themselves.

Aerial survey involves the recording of archaeological sites and monuments by photography from the air and the plotting and analysis of the results. Aerial photography is an important archaeological tool for two reasons: it can allow us to see archaeological sites that have not survived above ground, but where enough remains below ground to affect the growth patterns of surface vegetation; and it can allow us to 'stand back' and get a clearer picture of elements that are not obvious when seen from ground level. In any normal year, for example, buried walls can promote lines of reduced growth in a crop, while ditches result in increased growth. In a year of drought the pattern is enhanced. Similarly, the low shadows cast by slight undulations in a field can, when viewed from above, form themselves into a map of past building foundations or routeways. RCAHMS has a dedicated programme of aerial survey that can take advantage of specific flying conditions and build up a portfolio of photographs. With the aid of computers, many of the photographs can now be transcribed onto maps which can make them easier to understand and use.

For more recent times it is also important to remember that there is, of course, a shift in emphasis from the grass-covered humps and bumps of archaeology to upstanding buildings. For this reason an important part of RCAHMS is the architectural section who deal with the survey of buildings and monuments. Although much of their work is devoted to the remains of the relatively recent past, they also have an important role to play in the recording of earlier material.

The architectural survey that is undertaken by RCAHMS is divided into three programmes: threatened buildings survey, industrial survey and thematic survey. In addition to a consideration of the architectural and social merit of a building RCAHMS is also interested in the condition of the building. Alteration, redundancy and decay are all regarded as material to a building's interest, as well as any threat of demolition. In some cases there may already be an archive of material, usually including photographs and drawings, that relates to a building; in other cases the surveyors have to start from scratch. While photography is very useful, the surveyors' work often includes measured drawings and documentary research.

The threatened buildings survey considers buildings that are under threat of destruction or serious material change, whether through decay or deliberate alteration. It does not only deal with the grandiose remains of industry or upper-class living. Like the archaeological record one of the great assets of the RCAHMS architectural survey is that all buildings, whether small or large, may be considered. Work in recent years has thus included telephone boxes, public lavatories and small dwellings, as well as castles and churches.

The industrial survey deals with the record of all aspects of Scottish industry, both heavy such as engineering plants, and light such as commercial buildings. This work has come to be recognized as of particular importance given the very great changes that have taken place in the economic base of life in Scotland in recent years. Whereas gas cooling towers, pit heads and engineering works were once a familiar part of the Scottish landscape, their place has largely been taken by other, lighter industries, and so it is important to record the changing nature of the industrial scene. The industrial survey does not only record sites as they disappear, it also works to make a record of living industries and their processes. In this way video recordings, oral history and current papers are all used so that the archive comprises as up to date a record as possible.

The thematic survey looks at particular types of building, such as bridges or lighthouses, as well as material from specific geographical areas, such as St Kilda. Survey work, photography and other methods of recording are all important here. In many cases this work leads to specific exhibitions, as well as thematic publications (e.g. Hay & Stell 1986).

All of this recording work has resulted in the build up of a huge archive. This archive contains a wealth of information relating to the archaeological and historical heritage of Scotland, but housing and maintaining it is a very specialized task. This task is the responsibility of the National Monuments Record for Scotland (NMRS). The origins of the NMRS go back to the foundation of the Scottish National Buildings Record (SNBR) in 1941. This was set up to make an emergency record of the historic architecture of Scotland: given the vagaries of war there was a general recognition that many ancient buildings might not survive undamaged. The emergency record included collections of any existing architectural drawings that could be found as it was realized that this would be a rapid means to create a record of as many buildings as possible. The RCAHMS also carried out emergency surveys during the war years in areas that were likely to be damaged or taken into cultivation during the crisis. By the 1960s it was realized that the work and collections of the SNBR could be more effectively managed by amalgamation with those of the RCAHMS and the NMRS was formed, reflecting a call for national records that took place across the UK. The collections of the SNBR and the RCAHMS were combined and the work of the NMRS henceforth included information relating to all sites and monuments, prehistoric as well as historic, and earthwork as well as stone.

The NMRS today provides the public with access to a vast wealth of information and archive material relating to the architectural and archaeological history of Scotland. Photographs make up a substantial part of the collection, but there are also written records, drawings, architects' plans, old and new books, maps, video tapes, audio tapes, and more recently, electronic media. Material is added daily, not only from the RCAHMS survey work, but also from a great number of outside sources, both professional and public. Material is deposited in the NMRS by businesses, architects' practices, by individuals, and by professionals working in the field of architectural recording and archaeology. Professional archaeologists, for example, have a duty to collate the archive created during all fieldwork or excavation work that that they undertake. In Scotland, these archives are normally transferred to the NMRS where they can be properly stored, catalogued, and made available for future research. In this way, future generations will be able to make use of the raw data collected during work on a site that may no longer exist. In 1983 the annotated maps and associated records of the archaeology branch of the Ordnance Survey (OS) for Scotland were transferred to the NMRS, together with the responsibility for revising and updating the 'antiquity' information shown on all scales of OS published maps.

These records are at the heart of the Royal Commission and they are now seen as providing an inventory of sites, the purpose for which the RCAHMS was originally set up in 1908. This is a dynamic and accessible inventory which provides a resource that can be used by those with an individual or a professional interest alike.

The maintenance of a record of this size is not undertaken lightly. The NMRS employs specialist staff who ensure that the material created during RCAHMS field survey becomes available through the NMRS for general use. These staff are responsible for the cataloguing and good maintenance of the collections and they ensure that there is good public access to information. Specialist conservation treatment is required for some of the items in the collection, like plans drawn on tracing paper or old film, to ensure that they can be stored in a stable condition. Different types of environmental conditions are used to ensure that the collections are maintained in the best storage conditions for the various types of material that they contain.

Cataloguing is a vital part of the work of the NMRS to ensure that the information and items held in the collections are easily retrievable for public use. At the time of writing, there are approximately 150,000 site records, with over two million items in the collections. In 2000 some 14,000 people consulted the NMRS.

CANMORE, the Computer Application for National MOnuments Record Enquiries, provides on-line access to the NMRS database (http://www.rcahms.gov.uk, follow links to CANMORE). The information in this database provides basic details about many sites and buildings as well as information relating to the NMRS holding on that site. It is thus a useful resource of descriptive information as well as a first port of call for those who are considering a visit to the Record. The information held in CANMORE can be very technical and it is constantly being updated, so it is a changing resource for which the inexperienced user may need some guidance, but help is freely available from the NMRS, and CANMORE is unparalleled. It also provides links to relevant sites, such as SCRAN (the Scottish Cultural Resource Access Network).

Many people visit the NMRS in person, but for those who are unable it is also possible to consult the records on-line, through the CANMORE database, or through telephone calls, fax, and emails. Over 40,000 enquiries were made to CANMORE in 2000. However the request is made, the NMRS staff are on hand to help, and there is plenty of space for research as well as provision for the copying of information. The NMRS is a veritable treasure house of information relating to the past of Scotland, including both archaeological and architectural data as well as aerial photographs. In recent years the collections have been augmented by the acquisition of various series of aerial photographs so that the NMRS can now offer access to well over one million aerial photos and negatives relating to Scotland.

The NMRS is an important public resource, but it is little known. It is a wonderful source of old records and photographs, as well as of up-to-date information. This book concentrates on just one aspect of its holdings: photographs relating to archaeology. The photographic holdings of the NMRS are extensive, covering the whole of Scotland and dealing with every period of the past. Picking out suitable pictures for this volume, and whittling them down to a manageable number, was no easy task.

10 CONCLUSIONS

This book has not set out to be comprehensive, and readers may well have identified gaps in the photographic coverage and in the discussion. My intention has been to give an idea of the wealth of archaeological remains that exist in the countryside and of the ways in which they contribute to our understanding of the past. If you have spotted a gap you have clearly got a feeling for the type of archaeological sites and information that I feel are so interesting. Hopefully I have shown the great variety of sites and work that may be defined as 'archaeology'.

This book should have given the idea that archaeology is not just about the sites which are preserved and interpreted for the casual visitor. These represent only a tiny proportion of Scottish sites. Archaeology is about more than mere visits to manicured remains; it is much wider than that. It is about the countryside as a whole, and it is about the ways in which people have made use of it. Archaeology is about the ways in which the actions of the past pervade every facet of our lives today. It is an issue that touches all of us — in all that we do and wherever we go. If we can begin to understand what has gone on before us, how much better we can understand ourselves and our world. Archaeology is about our definition of ourselves and of the world in which we live.

Rather than getting bound up in the archaeological details of who did what in the past, and when, it is more important today to be aware that neither the landscape, nor our use of it, is static. Change is an inevitable process. It is change that takes us forward and makes sure that we can deal with the needs of tomorrow. Change is not something to be despised, and we cannot halt it, but it is something to be taken seriously, in particular its effects on the landscape. Change needs to be controlled. Unregulated change, and deliberate change that is not based on sound knowledge, are the harmful elements that we should seek to minimize.

Change should be carefully thought out and designed to make something positive for the future. If we seek to understand change and to manage it, it need not be a negative process. Nevertheless, we have a problem today in that the pace of change has greatly accelerated and this makes it harder to control than ever before. The scale of development with which we are dealing is usually such that in most cases the preservation of all traces of the past as they are written in the countryside cannot be upheld. We can only consider the preservation of remains that are regarded as of particular interest or worth. This is a difficult concept to put into practice as sites must be prioritized, for example on the basis of rarity, or on the basis of their quality of preservation to such an extent that they are of great importance. It is important to document sites and their alterations so that we do not lose the record of that which has gone before.

Even where ancient elements of the landscape have been lost, that landscape is not without interest if we have a thorough knowledge of its history. This is one of the roles of the archaeologist. Archaeologists seek to record sites that are under threat, whether from natural, animal, or human agency. Thus a treasure house of detail on past remains has been, and is being, collected. In this way the archives of the NMRS are built up.

Change does not just concern physical alteration; it is also a mental process and this is another aspect of our relationship with the land. The ways in which we look at the countryside today are very different to those of the past. A combination of topography with the present-day reliance on motorized transport means that in a few hours we can now reach places that were once considered remote. On the other hand, some of the places now regarded as remote were once at the heart of things. Roads and rail cannot reach everywhere and though they have speeded up the means of transport, they have limited its scope. The demise of the Clyde steamers, for example, has reduced the role of places like Campbelltown and Rothesay as an easily accessible recreation ground for the population of Glasgow. Further back in time, a network of seaborne transport provided strong links along the west coast of Scotland. This lasted for many millennia from the incursions of the first inhabitants after the Ice Age some 10,000 years ago, well into the establishment of the Lordship of the Isles just under 1000 years ago. Places like Islay, Rum and Applecross were not remote then.

Today great emphasis is placed on time. Time has been turned into an important commodity, but this was not always so. We have less time for travel. We want to arrive quickly, and this has affected our perceptions of remoteness and the technology of transport, as well as the management of change.

Altered perceptions of scale do not only affect distance and time. The industrial centres of the past, like Den of Boddam or Isle of Fethaland, would scarcely be considered industrial by the standards of today. Forestry has moved from a natural land use, through a cultivation practice, to an industry. Some sites, on the other hand, have moved from industry to leisure, for example Wanlockhead. At the same time, none of these divisions are clear-cut and different landscapes may mean separate things to individuals. One person's industrial nightmare may be another's conservation rarity, as shown by the debates on the preservation of the oil-shale bings with their quirky flora and fauna.

These are serious points with regard to the process of prioritization, for we tend to ascribe importance to places in relation to our values today. All too often, however, these are based on little evidence of past worth. To overemphasize ease of access, for example, can be an unhelpful distortion of the face of the land. The ascription of merit is a vital part of the building of priorities, but it is a dangerous and a difficult principal to operate. We can see how our understanding of the land has changed with time. The priorities of today are in danger of ignoring the needs of tomorrow.

Across Scotland, landscape change is managed through the application of policy. There are, however, limited resources to deal with this. It is hard for any agency to set aside adequate funds and so priorities have to be drawn up and implemented. If they are to be effective, these priorities need to be based on a sound knowledge of the existing elements of the countryside, including archaeology. The contribution of the past has perhaps been undervalued in recent years, but it is an important contribution, nonetheless. It provides the foundations to our understanding of the state of the land today as well as a guide to possible mechanisms of change and development in the future.

A proper understanding of the development of the landscape highlights the weakness of basing policy on a shallow regard of present-day worth. Landscape management should not be just about spectacular undeveloped areas, nor should it only concern rarity. Agricultural, urban and industrial perspectives are all integral parts of the landscape of Scotland. And they have not been static. The changing nature of land use means that even the most urbanized landscape of today was once rural (as demonstrated by the cultivation remains in Holyrood Park at the heart of the city of Edinburgh). Some of our wildest and most remote land, in contrast, was once land of great industrial value, often known for ease of access (Cluan; Furnace).

Policy making and implementation is not easy, and those who work on it rely on the compartmentalization of the landscape to assist them. This is difficult: not only is there change with time, but individual categories of landscape rarely exist in isolation. Domestic settlements sit at the heart of industrial vistas as at Kames. Swathes of agricultural land often incorporate the dwellings of those who worked there, for example Harris in Rum. The small size of the country, relatively intensive land use, and limited funds, have meant that land management policies are often drawn up and implemented patchily with different scales of intervention, or non-intervention, for individual areas. The appropriate scale of management for any one area is decided for a number of reasons, a major element being the perceived value of that area in the terms of the policy. Agricultural policies therefore tend to be more intensively applied in fertile and accessible areas, while conservation policies are operated in areas that are often more remote for us today and perceived as of greater 'natural' or 'wild' value.

Commercial Forestry provides a good example of landscape change that was not at first thought through. Initially, large-scale but simple afforestation was embraced as providing for both the needs of the present (making use of areas of 'wilderness') and the needs of the future (the provision of timber). Cultivation usually comprised the use of limited species of fast-growing non-native trees that were densely planted and cropped. The problems that arose from this affected many different aspects including archaeology. The use of new technologies meant that trees could be planted and harvested in areas that had previously been regarded as unripe for development so that little was known about their archaeological history. Wide tracts of archaeological remains were destroyed with little attempt to understand the past history of the land. There was little information about past vegetation and cultivation practices, and this led to its own problems. With time erosion took place and species loss among the native flora and fauna of the afforested areas became apparent.

Forestry today is a greatly altered process. It now encompasses more forethought and study. A greater variety of trees are planted, and both planting and felling techniques are adapted to suit the terrain. Provision for archaeological and other surveys in advance of afforestation is statutory. Forestry today is moving towards a practice that is more rooted in an understanding of the landscape and its past. It is, however, a good example of the complexity of the issues with which we are faced as we move into the twenty-first century. Is forestry an industry, or a conservation science? Does it comprise a type of agriculture?

Do forests provide a ritual landscape for the city-dweller of the twenty-first century? What scale of tree cover is appropriate? Popular movements celebrate the power of trees and wish to return Scotland to a density of native woodland that pre-dates any settled human occupation of the land.

It is important to realize that we can never recreate the world of the past. Though native trees are once again regarded as an important element of the landscape of Scotland, our concerns are very different to those of our predecessors. The result is that the new forest developments are quite different to the ancient woodlands. Most ancient woodland was actively managed, using techniques such as coppicing, in order to provide a variety of timber for different needs while maintaining steady growth to ensure future supplies. The provision of deadwood for fires, browse for animals, and clearings for cultivation were important issues. The needs of today are quite different, as is the pattern and density of population. Though Scotland has swung back to a reappraisal of native woodland, it will be a while before the ancient management skills that benefited both woodlands and people can be adapted to serve the needs of today.

To complicate the role of archaeology in the landscape, our knowledge of the past is not consistent. Just as there are great differences in scale between sites, so there are differences in our knowledge of different areas of the country. It is all too easy to make simplistic equations between size and interest, between visible remains and available information, and between knowledge and importance. But are they valid? What ought we to make of an isolated hut-circle such as that at Druim Mór? How much more interesting is it when regarded in conjunction with the cultivation remains that lie nearby? How should the relative merits of a small dun like Dunan nan Nighean be compared with a large fort such as Dùn Nosebridge? How does a barely-visible groove in the grass, as at Hill of Alyth, compare with upstanding stone remains like Gruting School? How should we equate management of the rich and well-documented ceremonial landscape of central Orkney with that of the less well-studied landscape at Ardnacross? How little we know of the Neolithic homes of central Scotland compared to those of the Northern Isles of Orkney and Shetland. These questions affect all who deal with archaeology in the landscape: whether at central government level or local level; whether they earn their living from it, or use it for relaxation. There is plenty of work to do.

Archaeology has still to fill many of the gaps that are needed to inform general management policy. In turn, management cannot be driven by archaeological need alone. It is an issue that concerns a wider range of interests. Only in this way can appropriate priorities be worked out to deal with the variety of landscapes and professions that go together to make up the Scottish countryside. Policy making is a difficult process that involves both integration and compromise, as can be seen in the current National Parks debate.

A good example of the weaknesses of the ways in which we make and implement land management policy today lies in the island of Rum. Rum is a National Nature Reserve managed by Scottish Natural Heritage. It is renowned for its natural facets such as geology, flora and fauna, and it has received many international accolades. At the same time, it is generally recognized that Rum contains many archaeological sites of great interest, some of which are recorded as outstanding in Scotland. The management of Rum today concentrates on nature conservation and it has been ascribed great wild land importance. The individual archaeological sites on Rum, however, when looked at in relation to one another, tell a very different story. Rum is one of the best examples in Scotland of a cultural landscape. This book contains three examples of the quality of cultural remains that survive on Rum: Harris, Orval and Kinloch.

The archaeological sites of Rum provide a fantastic document regarding changing human activities on the island over a period of some 10,000 years. The landscape of Rum today is so because of the actions of the generations that have lived and worked here. The inhabitants of Rum began to remove the woodland some 5000 years ago; they organized communal deer hunts 500 years ago; they maximized the fertile land with lazy-beds 250 years ago; they set up sheep farms, deer parks and salmon runs 150 years ago; and 50 years ago they turned the island over to nature conservation. In the course of this they left domestic sites, fortified sites, burial mounds, ceremonial areas, industrial sites, and great swathes of cultivation remains. There are few places in Scotland where such an intense, complex record has survived in its entirety without recent intervention. Rum is a true example of the way in which it is the interaction between sites, and between the archaeology and the rest of the landscape, that provides meaning to our interpretation of the ways of the past. This is vital if we are to understand the land as we know it today.

Of course Rum does have outstanding value in terms of nature, but there is no part of the island that has been untouched by human hand. From the reintroduction of sea eagles in the twentieth century to the ongoing plantation of native woodland, people are responsible for most of the acclaimed natural elements of Rum. The management of Rum is therefore a much more complex matter than prioritizing the welfare of its 'natural' elements. The tale to be told by the book of Rum today is such that very sensitive management is necessary in order that the individual threads are not threatened by future developments in any one field. The quality of the landscape as a whole means that Rum is one of the rare cases where it might be worthwhile to work towards preserving the landscape of today as a unique record of 10,000 years of human history.

Rum's special status as a Reserve means that integrated preservation should be possible. Unfortunately it is not so easy while we divide our management schemes (and officers) into those that deal with nature conservation and those that deal with cultural preservation. To date, the management of the archaeological sites on Rum has been carried out on the basis of the value of individual sites to archaeology in general. It has not been truly integrated into the management of the island as a whole. But it is only through a consideration of sites in context that they may be understood and management can move forward.

Landscape management is a complex issue that must be implemented through the application of a flexible policy designed to adapt to the changing needs of different areas of the country. Archaeology is only one of the elements that should be brought to play in the construction of this policy. It has, however, a vital part to play if we are truly to understand the depth of the land which we are trying to take forward into the future. Hopefully this book has given an idea of the wealth of material remains that survive, often hidden, in the countryside. Together with other remains, destroyed but recorded, these provide the foundation for our knowledge of the past. The application of this knowledge is manifest in a proper understanding of the past processes that have gone into the make-up of the countryside. Successful management has to be about the integration of this knowledge with information from other elements such as geology, flora and fauna as well as with the constraints of the present and needs of the future. Only in this way can we be sure that the landscape of the future is in safe hands.

BIBLIOGRAPHY

Books

Two series of books provide excellent background information to Scottish archaeology and history. *The Making of Scotland* series, published by Canongate with Historic Scotland, provides a well-illustrated introduction to the main periods of prehistory and early history. More detailed books covering the more recent historical periods as well as the early periods are published by B.T. Batsford and Historic Scotland. In addition, the *Exploring Scotland's Heritage* series of books, published by RCAHMS together with Mercat Press, provides a good geographical guide to a wide variety of sites of interest and puts them into their broader context. Books with specific information relating to the text are listed below.

Armit, I. 1998, *Scotland's Hidden History*. Stroud: Tempus

Bowden, M. (ed.) 1999, *Unravelling the Landscape*. Stroud: Tempus

Breeze, D.J. 1998, *Historic Scotland, 5000 Years of Scotland's Heritage*. London: B.T. Batsford

Council for Scottish Archaeology 2001, *The Archaeological Resource and the Historic Environment: Balancing Conservation with Development*. Edinburgh: The Council for Scottish Archaeology

Hay, G.D. & Stell, G.P. 1986, *Monuments of Industry, an illustrated record*. Edinburgh: the Royal Commission on the Ancient and Historical Monuments of Scotland

Love, J. 1983, *The Isle of Rum, a Short History*. Privately printed

MacSween, A. & Sharp, M. 1989, *Prehistoric Scotland*. London: B.T. Batsford

Magnusson, M. 1997, *Rum: Nature's Island*. Edinburgh: Luath Press

Menzies, G. (ed.) 2001, *In Search of Scotland*. Edinburgh: Polygon

Miket, R. 1998, *Glenelg, Kintail and Lochalsh, Gateway to the Isle of Skye*. Skye: Maclean Press

Mitchison, R. 1982, *A History of Scotland*. London: Methuen

Murray, D. 1958, 'Who Invented the Hot Blast?', *The Scotsman* (9 June). Edinburgh

Nicholaisen, W.F.H. 1976, *Scottish Place-Names*. London: B.T. Batsford

RCAHMS 1990, *North-east Perth: an Archaeological Landscape*. Edinburgh 1990: Royal Commission on the Ancient and Historical Monuments of Scotland

RCAHMS 1991, *National Monuments Record of Scotland Jubilee: a guide to the collections*. Edinburgh: The Stationery Office

Ritchie, A. 1985, *Exploring Scotland's Heritage: Orkney and Shetland*. Edinburgh: The Stationery Office

Ritchie, G. & Ritchie, A. 1992, *Scotland, Archaeology and Early History*. London: Thames and Hudson

Strachan, R. 1995, 'Auchenlaich Caravan site, Callander, watching brief and trench inspection', *Discovery and Excavation in Scotland*, 1995, 14

Walker, B. & Ritchie, G. 1996, *Fife, Perthshire and Angus*. Edinburgh 1996: The Stationery Office

Websites

BRITARCH	http://www.britarch.ac.uk/
CANMORE	http://www.rcahms.gov.uk
Council for Scottish Archaeology	http://www.scottisharchaeology.org.uk
Gask Ridge	http://www.romangask.org.uk
Historic Scotland	http://www.historic-scotland.gov.uk
National Museums of Scotland	http://www.nms.ac.uk/
RCAHMS	http://www.rcahms.gov.uk
SCRAN	http://www.scran.ac.uk

INDEX

Other titles published by The History Press

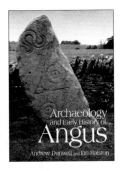

Archaeology and Early History of Angus

ANDREW DUNWELL AND IAN RALSTON

This accessible and well-illustrated overview of the archaeology of Angus concentrates on the period from the late Bronze Age to the rise of the Scots, broadly 1000 BC–AD 1000. The earlier prehistory of the area – from hunter-gatherer times onward, is also introduced. It sets the evidence for the settlements and burials examined in the new fieldwork alongside the classic site types of this part of eastern Scotland – including souterrains, vitrified and other hillforts, and Pictish sculptured stones.

978-0-7524-4114-6

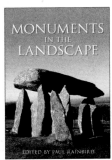

Monuments in the Landscape

EDITED BY PAUL RAINBIRD

Monuments in the landscape take many forms. This book brings together some major studies on the subject, including prehistoric sites fom south-west England, Romano-British remians from Salisbury Plain, medieval sites from Sutton Hoo, and post-medieval and modern monuments from the Scottish Highlands. Connecting them all is an appreciation of the archeological signatures in the landscape as monuments to human endeavour.

978-0-7524-4283-9

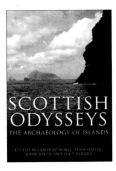

Scottish Odysseys: The Archaeology of Islands

EDITED BY GORDON NOBLE, TESSA POLLER, JOHN RAVEN AND LUCY VERRILL

Islands in Scotland have been attracting the interest of archaeologists since the birth of the discipline. This authoritative volume investigates 'islandness' in art, literature and archaeology. Topics covered by these essays include Irish identity, Bronze Age metalworking, standing stones in Mull, the interaction between island communities and archaeology, Foula, Iron Age land administration, lairds' houses, the Mesolithic to Neolithic transition, Rathlin Island, Neolithic North Uist, and the mentality of medieval Scottish crannog occupation.

978-0-7524-4168-9

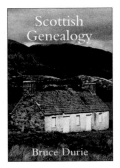

Scottish Genealogy

BRUCE DURIE

Scotland has possibly the most complete and best-kept set of records on the planet. Given both this and the fact that approximately 28 million people can claim Scottish ancestry, the lack of a thorough guide to Scottish genealogy is a significant gap. This book bridges that gap with authority and provides a sense of the excitement of the historical chase. Scottish Genealogy covers records and genealogical practice, and includes worked examples which will enable family historians everywhere to exploit the rich resources in Scotland.

978-0-7509-4568-4

Visit our website and discover thousands of other History Press books.

www.thehistorypress.co.uk